INTERVENTIONS

Conor Cunningham and Peter Candler

GENERAL EDITORS

It's not a question of whether one believes in God or not. Rather, it's a question of if, in the absence of God, we can have belief, any belief.

"If you live today," wrote Flannery O'Connor, "you breathe in nihilism." Whether "religious" or "secular," it is "the very gas you breathe." Both within and without the academy, there is an air common to both deconstruction and scientism — both might be described as species of *reductionism.* The dominance of these modes of knowledge in popular and professional discourse is quite incontestable, perhaps no more so where questions of theological import are often subjugated to the margins of intellectual respectability. Yet it is precisely the proponents and defenders of religious belief in an age of nihilism that are often among those most — unwittingly or not — complicit in this very reduction. In these latter cases, one frequently spies an accommodationist impulse, whereby our concepts must be first submitted to a prior philosophical court of appeal in order for them to render any intellectual value. To cite one particularly salient example, debates over the origins, nature, and ends of human life are routinely partitioned off into categories of "evolutionism" and "creationism," often with little nuance. Where attempts to mediate these arguments are to be found, frequently the strategy is that of a kind of accommodation: How can we adapt our belief in creation to an already established evolutionary metaphysic, or, how can we have our evolutionary cake and eat it too? It is sadly the case that, despite the best intentions of such "intellectual ecumenism," the distinctive voice of theology is the first one to succumb to aphony — either from impetuous overuse or from a deliberate silencing.

The books in this unique new series propose no such simple accommodation. They rather seek and perform tactical interventions in such debates in a manner that problematizes the accepted terms of these debates. They propose something altogether more demanding: through a kind of refusal of the disciplinary isolation now standard in modern universities, a genuinely interdisciplinary series of mediations of crucial concepts and key figures in contemporary thought. These volumes will attempt to discuss these topics as they are articulated within their own field, including their historical emergence and cultural significance, which will provide a way into seemingly abstract discussions. At the same time, they aim to analyze what consequences such thinking may have for theology, both positive and negative, and, in light of these new perspectives, to develop an effective response — one that will better situate students of theology and professional theologians alike within the most vital debates informing Western society, and so increase their understanding of, participation in, and contribution to these.

To a generation brought up on a diet of deconstruction, on the one hand, and scientism, on the other, Interventions offers an alternative that is *otherwise than nihilistic* — doing so by approaching well-worn questions and topics, as well as historical and contemporary figures, from an original and interdisciplinary angle, and so avoid having to steer a course between the aforementioned Scylla and Charybdis.

This series will also seek to navigate not just through these twin dangers, but also through the dangerous "and" that joins them. That is to say, it will attempt to be genuinely interdisciplinary in avoiding the conjunctive approach to such topics that takes as paradigmatic a relationship of "theology and phenomenology" or "religion and science." Instead, the volumes in this series will, in general, attempt to treat such discourses not as discrete disciplines unto themselves, but as moments within a distended theological performance. Above all, they will hopefully contribute to a renewed atmosphere shared by theologians and philosophers (not to mention those in other disciplines) — an air that is not nothing.

CENTRE OF THEOLOGY AND PHILOSOPHY

(www.theologyphilosophycentre.co.uk)

Every doctrine which does not reach the one thing necessary, every separated philosophy, will remain deceived by false appearances. It will be a doctrine, it will not be Philosophy.

Maurice Blondel, 1861-1949

This book series is the product of the work carried out at the Centre of Theology and Philosophy (COTP), at the University of Nottingham.

The COTP is a research-led institution organized at the interstices of theology and philosophy. It is founded on the conviction that these two disciplines cannot be adequately understood or further developed, save with reference to each other. This is true in historical terms, since we cannot comprehend our Western cultural legacy unless we acknowledge the interaction of the Hebraic and Hellenic traditions. It is also true conceptually, since reasoning is not fully separable from faith and hope, or conceptual reflection from revelatory disclosure. The reverse also holds, in either case.

The Centre is concerned with:

- the historical interaction between theology and philosophy.
- the current relation between the two disciplines.
- attempts to overcome the analytic/continental divide in philosophy.
- the question of the status of "metaphysics": Is the term used equivocally? Is it now at an end? Or have twentieth-century attempts to have a postmetaphysical philosophy themselves come to an end?
- the construction of a rich Catholic humanism.

I am very glad to be associated with the endeavours of this extremely important Centre that helps to further work of enormous importance. Among its concerns is the question whether modernity is more an interim than a completion — an interim between a pre-modernity in which the porosity between theology and philosophy was granted, perhaps taken for granted, and a postmodernity where their porosity must be unclogged and enacted anew. Through the work of leading theologians of international stature and philosophers whose writings bear on this porosity, the Centre offers an exciting forum to advance in diverse ways this challenging and entirely needful, and cutting-edge work.

Professor William Desmond, Leuven

HEIDEGGER

A (Very) Critical Introduction

S. J. McGrath

WILLIAM B. EERDMANS PUBLISHING COMPANY
GRAND RAPIDS, MICHIGAN / CAMBRIDGE, U.K.

© 2008 S. J. McGrath

All rights reserved

Published 2008 by

Wm. B. Eerdmans Publishing Co.

2140 Oak Industrial Drive N.E., Grand Rapids, Michigan 49505 /

P.O. Box 163, Cambridge CB3 9PU U.K.

Printed in the United States of America

14 13 12 11 10 09 08   7 6 5 4 3 2 1

Library of Congress Cataloging-in-Publication Data

McGrath, S. J., 1966-

Heidegger: a very critical introduction / S.J. McGrath.

p.   cm.   — (Interventions)

Includes bibliographical references.

ISBN 978-0-8028-6007-1 (pbk.: alk. paper)

1. Heidegger, Martin, 1889-1976.   I. Title.

B3279.H49M3756   2008

193 — dc22

2008006081

www.eerdmans.com

Contents

Preface

Slim postmodern introductory books like this one normally provide students with a summary. I interpret the task of introducing differently. The German word for introduction, *Einführung,* comes from *einführen,* which means "to lead someone in" (from the German *führen,* "to lead"). This book is not a summary but a leading into the subject matter. It is not intended to give newcomers Heidegger in a nutshell, in ninety minutes or less, and absolve them of the task of reading Heidegger. Rather, the book is designed to lead readers to Heidegger, from which point they will presumably begin or continue their own relationship with him.

For an introduction, this book is not always easy reading. Rather than following the increasingly popular "analytic" approach to Heidegger, which substitutes more commonly accepted philosophical terms for Heidegger's often torturous neologisms, I stick with Heidegger's language because it is inextricably related to the point he is making. If we are to understand anything of Heidegger, we need to engage, at least to a certain extent, in a hermeneutics of sympathy; we must allow Heidegger to temporarily reconfigure our concepts because it is only by such reconfiguration that Heidegger's way of seeing will open up to us, and it is precisely this way of seeing that is at stake.

Understanding Heidegger is like learning a foreign language: one inevitably begins disoriented, and only gradually, through trial and tribulation, does one find one's bearings. My sympathy, however, is held in check by suspicion. I have taken the "critical" qualifier of this "introduction" as an opportunity to raise some objections to Heidegger (which resolve in the end into one objection, the untenability of a methodological distinction between the ontological and the ontic); this both complicates and simplifies my task. It complicates it insofar as it drives me to speak about Heidegger at a level that will likely be too advanced for some readers; it simplifies it insofar as it allows me to uncover the axes of Heidegger's system of thinking, which might have otherwise required many more pages to expose.

It is worth noting that Heidegger has comparatively little to say about the ethical, political, and theological questions that are the foci of this critical introduction. In *Being and Time* the ethical is tabled for later ontic analyses; the political is scarcely mentioned; and the theological has so many qualifiers around it that we are discouraged from asking questions about it. These postponements are philosophically charged if not strategic. Ethical-political and theological issues have always already been decided in Heidegger (as they are in most philosophical treatises): the ontic/ontological distinction, Heidegger's justification for suspending ethical, political, and theological critiques of ontology, is a doomed effort to defer that which cannot be postponed.[1]

I wish to thank Conor Cunningham for suggesting this book; the Heidegger seminar of 2007 at Mount Allison University, which heard the first version of it; and Carol-Ann and Christina Galego for their encouragement and editorial assistance.

1. My approach to Heidegger's politics has similarities to the approach of the French sociologist Pierre Bourdieu. In *The Political Ontology of Martin Heidegger,* Bourdieu argues for a double reading of Heidegger that is both political and philosophical, pointing out that immanent readings of Heidegger, assuming a "sacred barrier between ontology and anthropology," have missed the essential connection between Heidegger's philosophy and his political activities. The political undertones do not invalidate *Being and Time* but prove it to be, like all texts, impregnated by the politics, economics, and history of its time. Heidegger is a case study of the impurity of every philosophical discourse. Pierre Bourdieu, *The Political Ontology of Martin Heidegger* (Stanford, Calif.: Stanford University Press, 1991).

Abbreviations of Heidegger's Works
with Original Dates of Publication

Where an English translation exists, I have referenced it and not the original German. For *Being and Time* I have given the pagination of the seventh German edition since that is found in the margins of both published English translations.

BDT   "Building Dwelling Thinking." 1954. In BW, 347-63.

BT   *Sein und Zeit.* 1927. 17th ed. Tübingen: Max Niemeyer, 1993. English translation: *Being and Time.* Translated by John Macquarrie and Edward Robinson. New York: Harper and Row, 1962.

BW   Martin Heidegger. *Basic Writings.* Revised and expanded edition. Edited by David Farrell Krell. New York: HarperCollins, 1993.

CT   *The Concept of Time. Begriff der Zeit.* 1924. German-English edition. Translated by William McNeill. Oxford: Blackwell, 1989.

GA1   *Martin Heidegger. Gesamtausgabe.* Vol. 1, *Frühe Schriften.* 1912-16. Edited by Friedrich-Wilhelm von Herrmann. Frankfurt am Main: Vittorio Klostermann, 1978.

GA5   *Off the Beaten Track.* 1935-46. Edited and translated by Julian Young and Kenneth Haynes. Cambridge: Cambridge University Press, 2002.

GA9   *Pathmarks.* Edited by William McNeill. Cambridge: Cambridge University Press, 1998.

GA16   *Martin Heidegger. Gesamtausgabe.* Vol. 16, *Reden und andere Zeugnisse eines Lebensweges.* 1910-76. Edited by Friedrich-Wilhelm von Herrmann. Frankfurt am Main: Vittorio Klostermann, 2000.

GA24   *Martin Heidegger. Gesamtausgabe.* Vol. 24. 1927. English translation: *Basic Problems of Phenomenology.* Translated by Albert Hofstadter. Bloomington: Indiana University Press, 1982.

GA56/57 *Towards the Definition of Philosophy.* 1919. Translated by Ted Sadler. New York and London: Continuum, 2000.

GA58   *Martin Heidegger. Gesamtausgabe.* Vol. 58, *Grundprobleme der Phänomenologie.* 1920-21. Edited by Hans-Helmuth Grander. Frankfurt am Main: Vittorio Klostermann, 1992.

GA60   *Martin Heidegger. Gesamtausgabe.* Vol. 60. *Frühe Schriften.* 1912-16. Edited by Friedrich-Wilhelm von Herrmann. English translation: *The Phenomenology of Religious Life.* Translated by Matthias Fritsche and Jennifer Anna Gosetti. Bloomington: Indiana University Press, 2004.

GA61   *Phenomenological Interpretations of Aristotle: Initiation into Phenomenological Research.* 1921-22. Translated by Richard Rojcewicz. Bloomington: Indiana University Press, 2001.

GA63   *Ontology and the Hermeneutics of Facticity.* 1923. Translated by John van Buren. Bloomington: Indiana University Press, 1999.

GA65   *Contributions to Philosophy (From Enowning).* 1936-38. Translated by Parvis Emad and Kenneth Maly. Bloomington: Indiana University Press, 1999.

ID   *Essays in Metaphysics: Identity and Difference.* 1957. Translated by Kurt F. Leidecker. New York: Philosophical Library, 1960.

IM   *Introduction to Metaphysics.* 1935. Translated by Gregory Fried and Richard Polt. New Haven: Yale University Press, 2000.

LH   "Letter on Humanism." 1947. In BW, 213-65.

PIA   "Phenomenological Interpretations in Connection with Aristotle: An Indication of the Hermeneutical Situation." 1922.

Translated by John van Buren. In *Supplements: From the Earliest Essays to* Being and Time *and Beyond,* ed. John van Buren, 111-45. Albany: State University of New York Press, 2002.

QT   "The Question concerning Technology." In BW, 307-40.

WM   "What Is Metaphysics?" 1929. In BW, 93-114.

CHAPTER I

Introducing Heidegger

If in this book I take the trouble to point out something essentially wrong with Heidegger's philosophy, it is only because there is so much that is right about it. Heidegger's phenomenological ontology was, in my view, the most vital philosophical development of the early twentieth century, an upsurge of philosophical eros in an era of bland positivism and dreary, inhuman reductionism. Heidegger set the tone for the way of proceeding with philosophy in the wake of the collapse of the great modern systems and the conquest of the natural scientific reduction of the human being. His critique of calculative thinking touched the nerve of modernity's obsessive-compulsive relationship with techno-science. His elucidation of the difference between the being of the human being (Dasein) and the being of everything else, perhaps his most lasting contribution, showed us, for the first time, how the tradition from Aristotle through Hegel defined the human being in terms borrowed from other beings: as a substance, or in its more modern variation, a subject — in both cases something with objectifiable properties. Heidegger was the first to point out that the existing individual has no properties because, unlike physical objects, it never exists as merely present and available for categorical dissection.

In the course of working out his vision of human existence and, on the basis of that, his doctrine of being, Heidegger makes certain ethical, political, and theoretical decisions *behind the scenes,* decisions that obstruct the task he sets for himself in his most fertile period of philosophical work, his early lectures and writings.[1] This task is nothing less than the grounding of ontology in a faithful analysis of everyday living. Owing to the nature of the subject matter — life, protean, elusive, and indefinable — Heidegger's goal is fidelity, not accuracy. The subject matter admits of no certainty or finality but demands an a priori commitment to possibility. Problems emerge when Heidegger forecloses certain phenomenological possibilities — stipulating in advance what is and is not possible for everyday being-in-the-world — by making a set of decisions unavailable for discussion or criticism. What protects these decisions from philosophical scrutiny is Heidegger's distinction between the ontological and the ontic, the existential and the existentiell, a distinction that is as essential to Heidegger's project as it is difficult for him to ultimately maintain.

Nonetheless, *Being and Time* remains arguably the best primer on phenomenology ever written. Those who study *Being and Time* do not merely read about phenomenology; they are thrown into it. If they persist with the unwieldy book, they catch a glimpse of how phenomenology works — a subject that is better caught than taught. There are many phenomenological analyses in *Being and Time* that are not obscured by Heidegger's unthematized prejudices. Critics who argue that the whole of Heidegger is Nazi ideology, or at best "a continuation of Nazism by other philosophical means," overstate their case.[2] Some go so far as to say that Heidegger's hermeneutics is intrinsically authoritarian and leads inevitably to totalitarianism. They argue that the model of truth as disclosure (in Heidegger's terms, *alētheia*) does not allow for the kind of public verification essential to democracy. To this one could reply that an *aletheic* doctrine of truth is not unique to Heidegger, but can be found in theories of truth throughout the history of philosophy. Plato and Aris-

---

1. On the young Heidegger, I have learned most from Theodore Kisiel's *The Genesis of Heidegger's* Being and Time (Berkeley: University of California Press, 1993).

2. The last phrase comes from Herman Philipse, *Heidegger's Philosophy of Being: A Critical Interpretation* (Princeton: Princeton University Press, 1998), 383. The most notorious of the witch-hunting books is Victor Farias's *Heidegger and Nazism* (Philadelphia: Temple University Press, 1989). Anyone interested in the facts of Heidegger's politics with a minimum of gloss should read Hugo Ott's *Heidegger: A Political Life,* trans. Allan Blunden (London: HarperCollins, 1993).

totle speak of *nous* as a sudden and nondiscursive vision of an indubitable principle. Aquinas speaks of *intellectus,* translated as "insight" or "intuition," as the presupposition of demonstrative reasoning. Hume and the empiricists refer to sensory impressions that are directly and unfalsifiably apprehended by the mind. More on the relation of *aletheia* to other intuitive models of truth later. For now the point is this: the task of the "very critical" interpreter of Heidegger is not to create generalizations that justify rejecting him *tout court,* but to identify the places in his phenomenology where the interpretation takes a questionable turn.

Heidegger's idiosyncratic language makes it difficult if not impossible to critique him from within his system of thinking because he deprives us of the terms necessary to challenge him. The language Heidegger requires us to speak is a language that endorses his view of things. This puts the critic in a difficult position: if the critic stays within an immanent critique, she risks losing critical distance; if she opts for a purely external critique, she risks failing to understand. A good example of the latter is Rudolf Carnap's critique of Heidegger's "What Is Metaphysics?" According to Carnap, Heidegger turns the logical structure of negation into a substantive, generating such senseless questions as "How is it with the nothing?" No serious student of Heidegger bothers with such critiques; too painfully do they miss the point.[3] Heidegger justifies his violence to German by arguing that language shapes thought; if ontology is to be rethought from the ground up, the old terms will need to be overhauled if not completely discarded. The point is well taken. To speak about being in terms of traditional binaries (substance and accident; essence and existence; cause and effect) is to frame thinking in such a way as to always miss the nonsubstantive, nonmechanical dimensions of ontology. On the other hand, to confine a critique of Heidegger to an immanent reading is to surrender our own voice. The Heidegger school that demands that we stay "within the text" enforces a rule that Heidegger himself would have never obeyed.

A major part of Heidegger's collected works consists of highly original "destructive" readings of the history of philosophy. Alongside the

3. Rudolf Carnap, "The Elimination of Metaphysics through Logical Analysis of Language," in *Logical Positivism,* ed. A. J. Ayer (Glencoe, Ill.: Free Press, 1931), 60-81.

works of Marx, Nietzsche, and Freud, Heidegger's interpretations of the pre-Socratics, Plato, Aristotle, Descartes, Leibniz, Kant, and Hegel belong to the literature of suspicion that gives the lie to consciousness.[4] The masters of suspicion disabuse us of modernity's naive confidence in reason. Modernity's faith in the rational and moral progress of European culture — the legacy of the Enlightenment — is shattered by Marx's discovery of the economic motive of Western culture; by Nietzsche's declaration of the will to power; and by Freud's exposure of the libidinous id operating behind our most civilized pursuits. Heidegger's contribution to the literature of suspicion is not as easy to encapsulate, but it is no less devastating. First he uncovers the interpretive nature of experience: we can no longer presume to have access to the things themselves unmediated by history and hidden prejudgment. Secondly he shows that Dasein is primarily motivated by self-deception, denial, and anxiety in the face of death, and that these "comportments" shape not only the way we see things but also the very things we see. The masters of suspicion suggest that reason is a puppet at the whim of something less than rational. For Marx, that something is capital and greed; for Nietzsche, it is hunger for power; for Freud, the inner lizard of repressed desire. For Heidegger, that something is the primordial, angst-driven flight from death: anxiety in the face of nothingness — the warp and woof of our sense of temporality — is the hidden motive underlying all our cultural, scientific, and religious achievements.

A hermeneutics of suspicion is necessary when reason is not in command of the discourse but is the product of "false consciousness." The most explicit example of how this works is classical psychoanalysis. In the Freudian model the analyst and analysand are not on equal footing. Assuming that the analysand is lying both to himself and to her, the analyst is primarily concerned not with what the analysand says but with how he says it. In the sutures of the analysand's narrative the analyst traces the hidden motives holding his illusion together. The relation is nondialogical, or one-sided. The analyst gives little of herself to the rela-

---

4. On Marx, Nietzsche, and Freud as masters of suspicion, see Paul Ricoeur, *Freud and Philosophy: An Essay on Interpretation,* trans. Denis Savage (New Haven: Yale University Press, 1970), 32-36.

tionship while the analysand must be trusted to hold nothing back if the cure is to work. It would not be appropriate for the analysand to break off the confession and say, "Well, I've told you about my mother — what about your mother?" The analysand is on trial; his language is not taken at face value. He is denied rationality, the ability to say what he means and mean what he says. His discourse is interpreted in light of assumptions that the analyst makes without telling him; his narrative is understood in terms of unconscious motives that are assumed to be revealed and concealed in the way he speaks or refuses to speak. Heidegger's readings of the history of philosophy proceed in a similar way: philosophers are not read at face value, but in light of assumptions they are presumed to have made but have not been able to thematize. Philosophy, for Heidegger, is symptomatic of Dasein's existential situation: Dasein's most quotidian struggles and anxieties may be seen at work in the most elaborate metaphysical systems. Instead of a history of competing efforts to understand being, Heidegger's reading of metaphysics presents a history of fictions constructed to avoid the truth of being.

Heidegger's approach to the history of philosophy, however, is never reductive or dismissive; on the contrary, it is marked by profound sensitivity to whatever is still alive in the concepts and occasionally brilliant exegesis. Hans-Georg Gadamer's philosophical hermeneutics stems directly from the style and method of Heidegger's early lectures on the history of philosophy, which Gadamer attended as a young philosophy student. There are many stories of the drama and intellectual electricity of Heidegger's lectures. Hannah Arendt speaks famously of "the rumor of a hidden king" of philosophy spreading among Freiburg students long before Heidegger became famous for writing *Being and Time.*[5] Philosophy was alive again in Heidegger's courses in a way it had not been since Hegel. Gadamer came upon Heidegger while writing his dissertation on Plato in the 1920s. Having heard the rumor in question, he dropped in on one of Heidegger's lectures. Heidegger was lecturing on Aristotle at the time, and Gadamer was astounded by what he heard. Heidegger lectured on Aristotle in a strikingly novel fashion, making bold new claims — an-

5. Hannah Arendt, "Martin Heidegger at Eighty," in *Heidegger and Modern Philosophy: Critical Essays,* ed. Michael Murray (New Haven: Yale University Press, 1978), 295.

chored in close textual readings — about the most widely discussed thinker in the history of Western philosophy. How could anyone say anything new about Aristotle?

Gadamer had witnessed a method Heidegger would come to describe as "violent interpretation." For Heidegger, philosophical interpretation must renounce fidelity to any so-called "literal" meaning of a text. The philosopher must discern which interpretations the text makes possible and which interpretations it conceals. The search for the author's intention as an incontrovertible criterion for interpretation is a red herring. We do not read an author's mind; we read an author's book. Even if we could somehow divine what the author has in mind, in the circles of historical finitude in which Dasein is thrown, the author has no more authority over the text's meaning than any other reader. What is at issue in interpretation is not what the author intends, but what the book is *about.* Gadamer noticed that Heidegger spoke about Aristotelian *phronēsis* as though Aristotle himself were in the room discussing the issue with Heidegger. For Heidegger, philosophical concepts are like living beings; they have their own historical career. Ideas are not dead matter to be examined objectively like bits of pottery or shards of bone; they show themselves to us in time, presenting ever new aspects of themselves. Neither do reading and interpreting alone draw us into historicity; human understanding, which Heidegger describes as a projection upon possibilities of being, is hermeneutical through and through (BT, 142-53). For Heidegger, the purpose of a lecture on Aristotle's *phronēsis* is to bring the phenomenon of *phronēsis* into being again. If it is hermeneutically sensitive to the situation of interpretation, the discussion will inevitably lead into areas that Aristotle could not have anticipated — because historicity, not Aristotle's "intention," has led the way.

After reading Jean-Paul Sartre's *Being and Nothingness,* which borrows heavily from *Being and Time,* Heidegger rejected the label "existentialism" (LH). But a cursory reading of division 1 of *Being and Time* shows that Heidegger is with some justification called an existentialist. In the ninth section of *Being and Time* Heidegger uses the words "essence" and "existence" in such a way that they short-circuit each other and can no longer be applied to human beings: "The 'essence' [*Wesen*] of this entity lies in its 'to-be' [*Zu-sein*]. Its Being-what-it-is [*Was-sein*] *(essentia)* must, so far as we can speak of it at all, be conceived in terms of its Being *(existentia)*" (BT, 42). Existence in the human sense is not the substantiation and instantiation of an essence; the essence of Dasein *is* its existence. Dasein is a kind of reverse image of the scholastic God (whose essence is also its existence). The scholastic God cannot not be; Dasein can never *simply* be. Its being is always outstanding, always yet to come. Dasein's "to be" is temporal, a being toward possibility: "*The 'essence' of Dasein lies in its existence.* Accordingly those characteristics which can be exhibited in this entity are not 'properties' present at hand of some entity which looks so and so and is itself present-at-hand; they are in each case possible ways for it to be, and no more than that. All the Being-as-it-is [*So-sein*] which this entity possesses is primarily Being. So when we designate this entity with the term Dasein, we are expressing not its 'what' (as if it were a table, house, or tree) but its Being" (BT, 42).

Existentialism sees philosophical significance in the emotional life of the human being, especially in feelings such as alienation, anxiety, boredom, and despair. For Heidegger, the state of being "thrown" into the world without a concept or word to explain it manifests itself in moods. In boredom and angst we feel the nothingness of our existence. Very much a mid-twentieth-century philosophy, existentialism thematizes modern dread in the face of sudden mass mobilization, technological warfare, and the dehumanization of urban life. It is relentlessly honest, painfully earnest, and inclined to political action. It is worth noting that the heyday of existentialism is past. Today we are apparently at home with *homo technologicus:* happy with our iPods and cell phones; awaiting the day when we can rid ourselves of even these clunky gadgets with the help of a microchip implant in the brain. We are all ironists and multitaskers, "saturated selves" comfortable in our bad faith. A few disenfranchised young people and left-wing intellectuals fuss about globalization, but when it is time to outfit a new home, the first stop for the majority is Wal-Mart, home of towering rows upon rows of cheap Asian-made products. We contentedly graze on fresh greens that have traveled a thousand miles; we savor Chilean Merlot. In the first half of the twentieth century, this brave new world of consumer oblivion was already on the horizon and was the subject of some concern. Intellectuals such as Oswald Spengler and Max Weber questioned whether mass culture, mass-produced goods, and technological organization were desirable things; Heidegger and the existentialists he inspired replied with an emphatic no.

Heidegger thought biography had little relevance for the study of philosophy. He once introduced a lecture on Aristotle with the bald statement: "He was born. He thought. He died." And yet Heidegger's own philosophy recommends the relevance of biographical interpretation. If the particular social and historical conditions determining a person's "being-in-the-world" are as essential to her understanding of being as Heidegger says they are, Heidegger's own biography is far from incidental to his understanding of ontology. Heidegger's diatribe against philosophical biography stands in open conflict with his general opposition to ahistorical approaches to philosophy. In contrast to Edmund Husserl, who in the early part of his career insisted on doing phenomenology without reference to the history of philosophy, Heidegger holds it necessary to first clarify the historical situation before endeavoring a phenomenological description. Understanding is not only mediated by history, it is constituted by it. The subtitle of one of Heidegger's first published writings, the preface to a book on Aristotle, is "Indications of the Hermeneutical Situation" (PIA). This peculiar text suggests an interpretation of Aristotle that is prefixed by a thorough overhaul of the historical concepts standing between the reader and Aristotle's text, in particular the legacy of Christian anthropology. Heidegger's task is not to remove these concepts (*Destruktion* is never that easy), but rather to show that our understanding of Aristotle is always mediated by traditional concepts. Bringing biography to bear on the interpretation of Heidegger is taking Heidegger at his word: Heidegger is as he was; he is his past.[6] He understands himself and everything else in terms of tradi-

---

6. Heidegger provides a phenomenological justification for the historical approach to philosophy in the first division of *Being and Time:* "In its factical Being, any Dasein is as it already was, and it is 'what' it already was. It is its past whether explicitly or not. And this is so not only in that its past is, as it were, pushing itself along 'behind' it, and that Dasein possesses what is past as a property which is still present-at-hand and which sometimes has after-effects upon it: Dasein is its past in the way of its own Being, which, to put it roughly, historicizes out of its future on each occasion. Whatever the way of Being it may have at the time, and thus with whatever understanding of Being it may possess, Dasein

tions of interpretation into which he has grown. He never naively assumes to be free of his history but rather believes that the meaning of his traditions lies always before him, coming to meet him from out of his future.[7] Heidegger's neologism for the being of the human being, "Dasein," means in German "being-there." The term is meant to preclude thinking about the subject as separable from his location in space and time, or better, his life situation. On the terms of Heidegger's own ontology, the "there" is crucial to understanding his philosophy, both in the "here" and "now" of the interpreter and in the "there and then" of the interpreted. Heidegger's language and words cannot be properly understood without reading his life, and reading it not merely from an ahistorical, objective perspective, but from a particular point of view.

Major works in the history of philosophy, however much they may appear to be the product of genius, do not drop out of the sky; they develop out of their times. The development of *Being and Time* from Heidegger's original plan — a book on Aristotle — to the massive monument to modern angst he ultimately produced was shaped by three popular movements in early-twentieth-century philosophy: neo-scholasticism, neo-Kantianism, and phenomenology. In spite of the paucity of references, especially to the first two, Heidegger could not have written *Being and Time* without these influences. On the biographical side, two well-known details of Heidegger's life help to shed light on the twists and turns of his "path of thinking": at one time in his life he was an enthusiastic Catholic seminarian trained in neo-scholastic philosophy; at another, he was an active member of the Nazi Party.

Heidegger's Roman Catholic upbringing shaped his ontological approach to phenomenology as much as his rural background shaped his political involvement with National Socialism. Heidegger was an active Roman Catholic until 1919, when he had an intellectual conversion to a

has grown up both into and in a traditional way of interpreting itself: in terms of this it understands itself proximally and, within a certain range, constantly" (BT, 20).

7. "Without this theological background I should have never come upon the path of thinking. But origin always comes to meet us from the future [*Herkunft aber bleibt stets Zukunft*]." Martin Heidegger, "A Dialogue on Language: Between a Japanese and an Inquirer," in *On the Way to Language*, trans. Peter D. Hertz (New York: Harper and Row, 1982), 10.

Protestant understanding of Christianity. In 1917 he married one of his students, Elfride Petri, a Lutheran, in a Catholic church service. After a year an expectant Elfride went to the priest who had married them, Father Engelbert Krebs, saying that she and Heidegger could not honor their commitment to baptize their child because her husband had lost his faith in the church, and she had not yet found hers. In 1919 Heidegger wrote a letter to the same priest (who was a close friend) describing his need to break from "the system of Catholicism."[8] He could no longer responsibly make his spiritual and intellectual home within the church. He would never feel comfortable with this break, and later in life he insisted that he "was never separated from the Church."[9] A few months before his death Heidegger met with a priest, his countryman, the Messkirch theologian Bernhard Welte. We do not know the details of the talk, but we do know that they spoke of Heidegger's relationship to the Catholic Church. In keeping with his request to Welte, Heidegger was buried in the Messkirch Catholic cemetery beside his parents and brother. At the end of his life Heidegger felt that Catholicism had a claim on him regardless of what he believed or what his intellectual objections might have been. He might not have subscribed to the beliefs of his fellow Catholics, but he was sure that his mortal remains belonged on Catholic soil.

Interpreting Heidegger's life through his own language, we could say that Heidegger was "thrown" into Catholicism. As such, his task was not to change his facticity (facticity cannot be changed) but to appropriate it and find an authentic relationship to it. Heidegger's father was the sexton of the church in Messkirch where Heidegger had served as an altar boy. Heidegger's childhood was punctuated by the liturgical year, with its rhythms of fast and feast and the mysteries of Christmas and Easter. Showing intellectual promise at a young age, Heidegger was handpicked by the local clergy for higher education. He attended a junior seminary, a

8. The letter is published in Ott, *Heidegger,* 106: "Epistemological insights applied to the theory of historical knowledge have made the system of Catholicism problematic and unacceptable for me — but not Christianity per se or metaphysics, the latter albeit in a new sense."

9. Heidegger, quoted in Thomas J. Sheehan, "Reading a Life: Heidegger and Hard Times," in *The Cambridge Companion to Heidegger,* ed. Charles B. Guignon (Cambridge: Cambridge University Press, 1993), 70-96, at 72.

grammar school for boys selected for the priesthood, where he was in-
structed in early scholastic philosophy and theology. The church was his
only ticket out of Messkirch; his family was too poor to finance his university education. Heidegger was anything but an unwilling novice. As a
student he wrote passionate articles defending the faith from modern
heretics. On his own initiative he tried to enter the Jesuit order, but was
turned down on account of his weak health. When he left for Freiburg to
study theology, he was still intent on life as a Catholic scholar if not as an
academic priest. Philosophy had been a passion for Heidegger since his
first encounter with it in grammar school. In 1912, two years before the
First World War erupted, Heidegger wrote a dissertation on logic, having
left his theological studies behind to pursue philosophy. Heidegger was
conscripted during the war, but his military duties were ultimately unde-
manding because he was recognized to have poor health. Stationed at a
meteorological post, Heidegger was responsible for telling the High
Command which way the wind was blowing — not unimportant infor-
mation in the days of gas warfare. The solitude afforded by being thus
isolated allowed Heidegger to continue his philosophical research,
which he devoted to his first book, his *Habilitationsschrift,* a second dissertation required of German scholars wishing to qualify for a teaching
position.

In Heidegger's lifetime neo-scholasticism dominated the Vatican as
well as many of the Catholic institutions with which his early career was
bound. Rejecting the antimetaphysical assumptions of modern philosophy, the neo-scholastics insisted that being was philosophy's most central
question. They rejected all historicist readings of the history of philosophy along with evolutionary or developmental theories of knowledge, arguing for a *philosophia perennis* that has remained largely unchanged
from Aristotle to the present day; the truth was held to be unchanging
and had been best expressed by Thomas Aquinas. The neo-scholastics
were not careful scholars of Aquinas, however, and substituted his original texts with philosophy manuals consisting of lists of theses and definitions. Training in this style of philosophy was essential to future priests
readying themselves for battle with the subjectivism of modernity, which
was the residue of what the neo-scholastics regarded as a steady philosophical decline that began in the High Middle Ages with the abandon-

ment of Thomism. The neo-scholastics believed that, cut off from being, philosophy could not but fall into the Kantian fallacy that reality revolves around the subject. When Heidegger broke with "the system of Catholicism" in his 1919 letter to Krebs, he referred to "insights applied to the theory of historical knowledge." A plausible interpretation of this passage is that Heidegger could no longer accept neo-scholastic ahistoricism.[10] From his early hermeneutics to his later "history of being," the notion that history determines our experience of truth is foundational for Heidegger: we understand as we are able according to our hermeneutical situation or epoch. Different ages of philosophy not only understand truth differently; they also have a different truth to understand.

Heidegger's qualifying dissertation is anything but a neo-scholastic study. Entitled *The Doctrine of Categories and Meaning in Duns Scotus,* it is an odd fusion of medieval logic with neo-Kantianism and phenomenology, and at the time it won little interest from scholars in medieval philosophy.[11] In it Heidegger attempts one of the first phenomenological readings of the history of philosophy. His approach was doomed to meet with disapproval from neo-scholastics, who associated the phenomenological movement with atheism and modernism. The book fared little better with phenomenologists. From their perspective, medieval philosophy was an epoch of theologically infected philosophy that scientific philosophers did well to avoid. Like many of Heidegger's youthful decisions, the choice of Duns Scotus for his qualifying dissertation was not without strategic intent. Heidegger believed that his future in academia lay in Christian philosophy. He had angled his dissertation in the hopes of catching the attention of the administration that would soon be re-

10. Carl Braig, the Freiburg theologian who mentored Heidegger as a theology student, should be mentioned here. Braig was an interpreter of the medieval tradition, but not a neo-scholastic. He encouraged Heidegger to read the primary scholastic sources, rather than the manuals, and bring scholastic concepts into discussion with modern philosophy. On Braig see John D. Caputo, *Heidegger and Aquinas: An Essay on Overcoming Metaphysics* (New York: Fordham University Press, 1982), 45-57.

11. Heidegger draws on authentic Scotistic texts as well as *De modis significandi* by Thomas of Erfurt, which he believed was written by Scotus. Martin Grabmann proved in 1922 that it was not. See Jack Zupko, "Thomas of Erfurt," in *The Stanford Encyclopedia of Philosophy,* ed. Edward N. Zalta, Fall 2006 ed., available at http://plato.stanford.edu/archives/fall2006/entries/erfurt/.

placing the chair of Catholic philosophy at the University of Freiburg. Moreover, the research for his book had been funded by a Catholic granting agency, one of whose stipulations had been that he remain faithful to the spirit of Thomas Aquinas.

In 1910, fearful of developments in biblical interpretation that appeared to challenge the fundamentals of the faith, Pope Pius X ordered professors at Catholic universities to swear an oath against modernism. Heidegger did not respond well to the edict, mocking with bitter irony the pope's authoritarian approach in a letter to Krebs: "Philosophical demand could be met by setting up vending machines in the train station (free of charge for the poor)"; "all who succumb to having independent thoughts could have their brains taken out and replaced with Italian salad."[12] Like many other Catholic intellectuals at the time, the young Heidegger resisted censorship and authoritarian intervention in scholarship even as he gave himself wholly to the Catholic intellectual enterprise. He found his path to fidelity in the honesty of scholarship. In his own words from this time, his work was dedicated to "researching and teaching Christian-Scholastic philosophy" and "making the intellectual riches stored up in scholasticism available and usable for the spiritual battle of the future over the Christian-Catholic ideal of life."[13] These are not empty words written to placate nosy administrators. In a handwritten curriculum vitae presented to the philosophy department in 1915, Heidegger described his "basic philosophical convictions" as "Aristotelian-Scholastic," adding that his next work would be "a comprehensive presentation of medieval logic and psychology in the light of modern phenomenology."[14]

Heidegger was crestfallen when the chair of Catholic philosophy was given to someone else in 1916. It was the second time the church had turned him down (he was first rejected by the Jesuits, when he sought entrance into their community at Tisis in 1909). In the year that followed he showed the first signs of a change in religious outlook — a volte-face perhaps not entirely unrelated to his professional disappointments. He immersed himself in Protestant theology, especially Schleiermacher and

12. Cited in Sheehan, "Reading a Life," 74.

13. These autobiographical statements by Heidegger date to the years 1914 and 1915. Cited in Sheehan, "Reading a Life," 74-75.

14. Cited in Sheehan, "Reading a Life," 75.

Luther, and in his notes and discussions began to attack the foundations of Catholic theology.

Heidegger worked on his Scotus book under the supervision of the neo-Kantian philosopher Heinrich Rickert. This alone would have alerted the Freiburg Catholic faction that Heidegger was doing something other than neo-scholastic research. Neo-Kantianism is an early-twentieth-century revival of Kant after a long period of the latter's eclipse by apparently more adventurous thinkers such as Hegel and Nietzsche. Neo-Kantianism downplays the metaphysical repercussions of Kant's critique, which had led to German idealism, concentrating instead on Kant's transcendental method. The neo-Kantian transcendental method can to some extent be seen at work in *Being and Time*. It involves a deduction of the epistemological and ontological "conditions of possibility" that must be the case given certain facts of experience. The method is empirical insofar as it begins with incontrovertible experiential data; it is transcendental insofar as it does not deduce hidden causes of known effects, but rather conditions of possibility that are of an entirely different order than facts. To use one of Kant's examples, space is the transcendental condition of the possibility of a three-dimensional object. Space itself is not a three-dimensional object; it cannot be directly experienced in the way a three-dimensional object can be directly experienced. We do not experience space as such; we experience the spatiality of things. If there were no bodies, there would also be no experience of space. Yet without space, three-dimensionality is not possible. In *Being and Time* Heidegger transcendentally deduces the meaning of being — temporality — from the fact that Dasein questions the meaning of being. Two years after *Being and Time* was published, Heidegger published a study of Kant's *Critique of Pure Reason* that justly earned him a reputation for being, if not quite a neo-Kantian, a Kantian scholar of considerable merit.[15] The book was taken seriously by Kant scholars and led to a famous debate, in 1929, between Heidegger and the neo-Kantian Ernst Cassirer. Heidegger advances a novel interpretation of *The Critique of Pure Reason* as a work of ontology rather than, as is usually assumed (even by Kant himself), a study of epis-

15. Martin Heidegger, *Kant and the Problem of Metaphysics,* trans. Richard Taft (Bloomington: Indiana University Press, 1990).

temology. Heidegger's unprecedented (and perhaps untenable) interpretation renders *The Critique of Pure Reason* one of the most important forerunners of *Being and Time*.

Heidegger's Scotus book, then, was undertaken not only to win the allegiance of the Catholic faculty at Freiburg but also to establish its author's neo-Kantian credentials.[16] The book is justly neglected by all but scholars of the early Heidegger; it is not a particularly good study of Scotus nor a particularly insightful neo-Kantian or phenomenological retrieval of medieval ontology. The significance of the work for understanding Heidegger's development greatly outweighs its value as a piece of scholarship. We witness how Heidegger was able to find a springboard in his Catholic studies for the questions motivating his first efforts in phenomenology. Heidegger homes in on a concept in Scotus that bears directly on the problem of time: Scotus's notion of *haecceitas,* the "formality" of individuality. Against Aquinas, Scotus argues that a thing is not individuated by matter, which is accidental to essence, but by a formal structure of difference shared with no other thing. *Haecceitas* literally means "thisness": it is the quality of every existing thing to be "this" and no other. *Haecceitas* cannot be defined because it is not subsumable under a species and a genus (the two elements in a definition according to Aristotle's logic); it is the essence of the thing in its most singularized existence, the essence insofar as it cannot be abstracted and generalized to apply to other things. Scotus's notion of *haecceitas* entails a theory of cognition that elevates intuitive knowledge (simple apprehension) above abstract knowledge. Insofar as it misses *haecceitas,* abstraction is at best approximate knowledge, at worst a distortion of the thing. Heidegger's interest in Scotus's critique of the derivative nature of abstract knowledge gives rise in his earliest lectures to his phenomenological critique of the theoretical attitude that forgets that the "fore-theoretical" richness of life can never be conceptualized in abstract terms. Heidegger writes that Scotus's *haecceitas* shows a keen sensitivity "to real life, to its manifoldness and possible tensions" (GA1, 203). In his 1919 lectures

16. Heidegger modeled his work after Rickert's star student, Emil Lask, who had written a similar neo-Kantian retrieval of ancient philosophy. On Lask, see Kisiel, *The Genesis,* 25-28.

Heidegger speaks of accessing the fore-theoretical by "hermeneutic intu-ition" of the forms of meaning that "live in life itself" (GA56/57, 117). While this is not exactly Scotus's notion of *simplex apprehensio* of *haecceitas,* the analogy between the two concepts is undeniable.

The Scotus book also shows how, from the beginning of his career, Heidegger belonged equally to two worlds of thinking: modern and premodern. In the introduction to the Scotus book he celebrates the me-dieval notion of intentionality as a successful avoidance of the Cartesian cleaving of the world into subject and object. And yet Heidegger does not simply immerse himself in the Middle Ages. Most of his secondary refer-ences are to neo-Kantian and phenomenological texts. Heidegger recon-nects modern philosophy to a certain premodern sensibility without abandoning modernity in the process. This dual emphasis on the mod-ern and the premodern stays with him throughout his long career; later he becomes equally preoccupied with the problems of modern technol-ogy and Greek philosophy. The Scotus book also shows why Heidegger was never to fit in among his neo-scholastic peers. Although raised and reared in an antimodern environment, Heidegger was far too involved with the problems of modernity to subscribe to the *philosophia perennis.* He had internalized from a young age the modern turn toward the sub-ject that begins with Descartes and ends in Nietzsche's "death of God." Unlike some of his contemporaries who shared his insistence on think-ing with modernity instead of against it, Heidegger was also steeped in premodern thinking: as a young man, in the medieval tradition; and later, in the ancient Greeks.

Heidegger met Husserl, "the father of phenomenology," in 1916 when the latter took a chair at the University of Freiburg — the chair that Heidegger himself would come to occupy thirteen years later. Heidegger had been reading the work of Husserl since his seminary days and had identified Husserl as a potential mentor, hoping to work as his assistant. Husserl was at first unimpressed with Heidegger, dismissing him as a Catholic intellectual, i.e., one who lacks enough freedom from religious indoctrination to engage in serious scholarship. Husserl, Jewish by birth, described himself as "a free Christian" and nondogmatic Protestant; he vigorously opposed any theological interference in phenomenology. It was only when Husserl had learned secondhand that Heidegger had experienced a dramatic change in religious orientation that the former invited the latter to work with him. In a 1917 letter to a colleague, Husserl announced that Heidegger had finally "freed himself from dogmatic Catholicism" and "cut himself off — clearly, energetically, and yet tactfully — from the sure and easy career of a 'philosopher of the Catholic worldview.'"[17] Husserl understood Heidegger to have undergone a religious conversion, the result of "difficult inner struggles" that precipitated "radical changes in [Heidegger's] basic religious convictions," and a turn to Husserl's particular brand of nondenominational Protestantism.[18]

We know from the few references that survive from his early study of Luther that Heidegger was particularly attracted to the Lutheran doctrine of *corruptio,* the deformation of human nature resulting from original sin. Luther rejects as naive and blasphemous the medieval scholastic anthropology summed up by Aquinas in the trope "Grace perfects nature, it does not destroy it."[19] For Luther, the history of salvation reveals that we are totally corrupt; in the wake of the darkening of the intellect and disorientation of the will, both of which are consequences of original sin, humanity can no longer be said to have a natural capacity for the truth. What we call the truth, in Luther's view, is actually falsehood because we no longer have a natural orientation to God. We suffer, on the contrary, from an aversion to God *(aversio Dei).* Luther's savage undercutting of reason is one of the earliest versions of the lying consciousness, the first hermeneutics of suspicion in the Western tradition. Luther believes that God himself reveals us to be self-deceptive. That the appearance of God on earth was possible only in the form of the crucified — God in a form opposite to his nature — is proof for Luther of the perversity and disorientation of reason. The crucified forces us either to reject God or to reject reason: faith alone can see God in the crucified. The young Heidegger became enthusiastic about this pessimistic reading of human nature: the dark tone, the profound suspicion of reason, confirmed his own postwar pessimism and inspired his defection from Catholicism and scholasticism. The Lutheran influence

---

17. Husserl, letter to Paul Natorp, cited in Sheehan, "Reading a Life," 76.
18. Husserl, letter to Rudolph Otto, cited in Sheehan, "Reading a Life," 76.
19. Aquinas, *Summa Theologica* (New York: Benziger Brothers, 1947), 1a, q. 1, a. 1.

explains in part why we find terms like "fallenness," "conscience," and "guilt" in *Being and Time*. Also worthy of notice is that God is not part of phenomenological experience for Heidegger. Luther rejects the scholastic notion of a *desiderium naturale*, a natural desire for God that can account for natural religion and philosophical theology, i.e., approaches to God that have never benefited from divine revelation. For Luther, any God that occurs to human reason independent of revelation is a construct designed to protect us from the truth. Luther would arguably approve of Heidegger's philosophy of authenticity, which is conspicuously devoid of religious reference. Elsewhere I have called this collusion with Luther Heidegger's "phenomenology for the Godforsaken." The Godforsaken are so fallen that they do not know they are fallen. Heidegger's phenomenology is an analysis of being-in-the-world for Lutheran man before he is given the faith that illuminates his existence as fallen, disfigured, and deceived.

Being and Time can be read as Heidegger's systematic defection from the "Christian-scholastic philosophy" to which he once swore allegiance. Heidegger's orientation to ontology — so novel in the early twentieth century, when the trend was increasingly toward epistemology and philosophy of language — is a residue from his training in medieval philosophy, especially under the theologian Carl Braig. Heidegger devotes little ink in *Being and Time* to the medieval ontological tradition he knew so well; this does not mean, however, that this tradition does not play a decisive role in his thinking. I have argued elsewhere that the Heidegger of *Being and Time* uses the language of ontology in such a way as to reverse central neo-scholastic theses.[20] Neo-scholastic ontology traces all philosophical questions back to the question of God. To answer any ontological question, the neo-scholastics insist that one must first attain some understanding of eternal being or pure act *(actus purus);* all other senses of being are defined in terms of God. Heidegger reverses this thesis in *Being and Time:* to answer any ontological question, Heidegger argues, one must first attain some understanding of time or temporality; all other

20. See my *The Early Heidegger and Medieval Philosophy: Phenomenology for the Godforsaken* (Washington, D.C.: Catholic University of America Press, 2006), chapter 1, "Heidegger and the Medieval Theological Paradigm."

senses of being are defined in terms of temporality. When ontology is temporalized in this way, God can no longer enter into it.

Through his exposure to Protestantism Heidegger became convinced that Christianity does not need metaphysics as a philosophical support (to argue otherwise is unbelief); Christianity has its own integrity, its own nonphilosophical foundations. Husserl's rule concerning the suspension of all God-talk in phenomenology[21] appealed to Heidegger on theological grounds. It followed for Heidegger that one needs faith rather than philosophy to understand Christianity; the phenomenologist can offer only external descriptions of religious phenomena — a necessary undertaking, to be sure, since all phenomena, according to Husserl, are equally in need of phenomenological analysis. In one sense Heidegger is simply being a good follower of Husserl when he "brackets" God from the phenomenological analysis in *Being and Time*. But whereas Husserl does this in a relatively neutral way, allowing for the coexistence of multiple theologies on the periphery of phenomenology, Heidegger's approach is hostile and subversive. Heidegger's phenomenology determines what is and is not possible for theology. As will be made more explicit in chapter 5 of this book, *Being and Time* is not theologically neutral, but conceals a hidden theological agenda: terms are defined in such a way as to make it impossible for philosophy to ask the God-question or for theology to use philosophy. It is not theologically insignificant that God appears nowhere in *Being and Time* — not even as a desire or cultural artifact. That Dasein has no natural religious life is an implicitly theological position, a rejection of the doctrine of natural theology.

Being and Time is a work of its time, heavy with the world-weariness and gloom of Germany between the wars. Max Weber's hugely influential 1918 lecture "Science as a Vocation" sums up the spirit of disillusionment, pessimism, and despair that gripped Germany after the First World War.[22] Weber points out that the old world has been buried with a generation of men dismembered in the trenches of France and that a new one is

---

21. See Edmund Husserl, *Ideas Pertaining to a Pure Phenomenology and to a Phenomenological Philosophy*, vol. 1, *General Introduction to a Pure Phenomenology*, trans. F. Kersten (The Hague: Nijhof, 1982), 173-74.

22. *Max Weber: Essays in Sociology*, trans. H. H. Gerth and C. Wright Mills (New York: Oxford University Press, 1946), 129-56.

yet to be born. Time-honored traditions such as Christianity, the Enlightenment, and the monarchy have failed. Instead of the promised utopia, science has delivered the bloodiest and most meaningless war in human history. Science has proven itself to be ethically and spiritually bankrupt, incapable of answering the most basic questions of human existence. Since religion is no longer an option for most intellectuals, Weber continues, Westerners no longer have a place to turn with their questions concerning the meaning of life. In a crowded lecture hall at the University of Munich in 1918, Weber proclaimed what everyone was feeling: the rationalization of society and culture that had been zealously pursued for over a century was nowhere near as enriching as it proposed to be; nor was the technologically reorganized Europe of the twentieth century necessarily a better or more humane society. Twentieth-century Western civilization, according to Weber, experiences meaninglessness on a scale that no previous culture has hitherto experienced: the meaninglessness of being without a cosmos. In the face of absurdity, at a time when reason has proven ineffectual at offering guidance concerning the most basic problems of human life, and religion is no longer a possibility, Weber asks, what role can science still play in culture? Weber's answer to this question touches the persistent will to knowledge that motivates the young Heidegger: if science cannot answer the ultimate questions of life, the one thing it can still do is examine itself and come to terms with its limitations and the inherent inconclusiveness of human living. Science can help us stay close to the truth of life, even if the truth of life is that it has no ultimate truth or ultimate resolution. In a Weberian key the early Heidegger believed that, after the collapse of reason, phenomenology could at least be faithful to its own task and give an open-eyed and fearless description of human existence in all its poverty and ambiguity.

In 1919 — the year Heidegger began to lecture at Freiburg as Husserl's assistant — old Germany was decisively put to death by the Treaty of Versailles. This tyrannical piece of victor's justice introduced war reparations that were so severe they ushered in a decade of economic chaos that laid the groundwork for the rise of Hitler. The early Heidegger's language, bristling with radicality, intensity, and urgency, belongs to this age. Held during an emergency war semester in 1919, "Philosophy and the Problem of Worldviews" (GA56/57; Heidegger's "breakthrough lecture" in the opinion of Theodore Kisiel)[23] is charged with the language of crisis and the call for a paradigm shift. Heidegger argues that the only way forward for philosophy is as phenomenology, but phenomenology in a sense quite different from Husserl's. In this first year under Husserl's tutelage, Heidegger criticizes his mentor for being overly theoretical. Introducing the theme of facticity, Heidegger calls for a phenomenology more sensitive to the fore-theoretical nuances of everyday life. In *Being and Time,* the Weberian apocalyptic tone becomes even more overt. The human being as Heidegger describes him, anxious, paralyzed by self-deception, wallowing and constantly losing himself in the mediocrity of the crowd, mirrors the German situation at the time the book was written. The imminence of a world-changing epochal decision had cast its shadow over Germany. Like Dasein, Germany was poised to decide in the face of the abyss to be itself or not, and in this decision it could expect no guidance from philosophy or theology, at least not in the traditional form of persuasive reasons for choosing one way over all others.

Still searching for a permanent teaching position, Heidegger took a job at Marburg University in 1923 as an associate professor. In this traditional stronghold of Protestantism, no longer under the scrutiny of a close-knit Catholic community, he could give free rein to his developing theological interests. He became an active participant in Rudolph Bultmann's New Testament seminars, giving lectures on Luther to Bultmann's theology students.[24] In his frequent discussions with the Marburg theologians, Heidegger referred often to Franz Overbeck's notion of "Christianness." Overbeck, a nineteenth-century theologian, understood the effort to theorize Christianity in terms of speculative and metaphysical theology to be a betrayal of Christianity's essence. Kierkegaard, Schleiermacher, Luther, and Overbeck became a chorus of voices in Heidegger's mind testifying to the degenerate nature of the medieval synthesis of philosophy and theology. Heidegger came to acknowledge that any attempt to unite these diametrically opposed dis-

---

23. Kisiel, *The Genesis,* 21.

24. The protocol from one of these seminars, "The Problem of Sin in Luther," has been translated by John van Buren in Martin Heidegger, *Supplements: From the Earliest Essays to* Being and Time *and Beyond* (Albany: State University of New York Press, 2002), 105-10.

courses would disfigure both beyond recognition. For Heidegger, theology is truly itself only when it stands in open conflict with philosophy (in the style of Luther or the early Karl Barth); philosophy resolutely does not believe.

In everything he did Heidegger remained the son of the Messkirch sexton. His conservative, agrarian values could not be concealed; indeed, he was proud of his humble roots. He was neither urbane nor cultivated, having descended from peasant stock, a heritage with which he identified throughout his life. Messkirch, where Heidegger was born and raised — and to which he would always return — is an unremarkable little village. In the town square stands St. Martin's Catholic Church, where Heidegger's father spent most of his years maintaining the property. The steeple, standing tall above the red-tile roofs of the townhouses, overlooks fields that stretch to the forests of the Swabian Alb. Heidegger's youth was spent wandering these fields and wooded hills. As a professor at Freiburg, he spent much of his time in his hut in the Black Forest, which Elfride had built for him in 1922. It was a mountain retreat where he could live and work in proximity to the elements without electricity, running water, and the other accouterments of modern life.

After the success of *Being and Time* in 1927, Heidegger was offered a prestigious professorship in Berlin. He turned it down and in 1934 gave a radio broadcast entitled "Why Do We Stay in the Provinces?"[25] The broadcast has a decisively political thrust appropriate to its historical moment: Heidegger shares his political vision for the new Germany then under construction by the Nazi Party, a vision according to which the people of Germany would rediscover their ties to their native soil. The German identity crisis to which Nazism was a response had, in Heidegger's view, as much to do with industrialization and the degradation of rural life as with the Treaty of Versailles. Heidegger describes an unlikely kinship between the academic philosopher and the worker of forest and field: if each remains equally dedicated and surrenders to his allotted task in life, the whole of society could expect to enjoy an experience of social unity stronger than that which any government or other

---

25. Martin Heidegger, "Why Do We Stay in the Provinces?" trans. T. Sheehan, in *Heidegger: The Man and the Thinker*, ed. T. Sheehan (Chicago: Precedent Press, 1981), 27-29.

organization could ever impose. The farmer goes to his field, the worker to his woods, and the philosopher (Heidegger) to his desk. At the end of the day they are at one in their weariness, yet content to have each been faithful to their own work. "Why Do We Stay in the Provinces?" echoes the transcendental ethics of *Being and Time,* articulating a right-wing vision of a society in which individuals contribute to the common good first by recognizing and responding to what is most properly their own *(eigentlich).* It was this conservatism and concern for rural Germany that made Heidegger sympathetic to the Nazis. We sometimes forget that National Socialism was not only about warmongering and racial purity, but was also founded upon a preferential option for the blue-collar worker, including an attractive policy of bringing Germans back into the fields and workshops and getting the nation working again. To the end of his life Heidegger's perspective remained a view from the countryside. His later concerns with the increasing role of technology in daily life were from the perspective of one who knew another way of living.

In the 1920s and early 1930s Germany was struggling with exponential inflation, spiraling unemployment, and an identity crisis. The shadow of the communist revolution, which had seemingly been successful in Russia, had fallen over Germany. Internationally supported efforts at establishing democratic structures — the Weimar Republic — met with little success. Communism horrified Heidegger. It struck him as a rationalistic and calculative effort to organize human society en masse, an effort that would undoubtedly entail the demise of the German nation. Having witnessed Germany's humiliation in the First World War, Heidegger was passionately interested in preserving and protecting the nation at all costs. The other global alternative, capitalism, was no more appealing to him; it too was born of a materialistic and positivistic view of culture and would just as surely destroy Germany. Heidegger believed that the fate of the West depended on the direction Germany took in this moment of decision. The German identity crisis had global significance; it concerned the future of the Western world. The National Socialist platform as it appeared in 1933 — centralize, militarize, restructure society with the worker at the center, and abolish the old hierarchies and aristocracies — was music to Heidegger's ears. Heidegger was never particularly interested in the racist agenda of the Nazi Party; anti-Semitism struck him as crude and biologistic. He could overlook this shortcoming, however, so long as what he felt were the deeper, spiritual springs of German unrest were addressed. The political radicalism and decisionism of the Nazis seduced Heidegger into becoming politically active for the first time in his life. In its hour of crisis Germany needed to be resolute — without any guarantees that any particular decision was the right one. Not to make a decision, however, was for Heidegger certainly the wrong course. Under Weimar, Germany had stagnated from too much reflection, mediation, and democracy. It was time for a change, and there was no political precedent for what needed to be done. Like Nietzsche's Overman, Germany needed to create new values in the void.

In 1933 Heidegger joined the National Socialism Party in Freiburg. This was initially an expedient move for him; it coincided with his assumption of the rectorship of the University of Freiburg, a position of significant political power at the time. In his office as rector Heidegger spearheaded the Nazification of the university, a process that involved inspecting professors and staff for their political correctness, firing Jewish colleagues, and overseeing the politicization of the knowledge industry. Heidegger never denied that he was for a time an enthusiastic enforcer of Nazi ideology.[26] Citing irreconcilable differences with the party, he resigned the rectorship after a year and retreated from politics. He spent the Second World War lecturing on poetry, language, and technology. Despite no longer being trusted by the Nazis, Heidegger never withdrew his membership from the party. When the allied British and American forces were bombing the medieval town of Freiburg into rubble in 1945, Heidegger was giving lectures on Hölderlin at a nearby castle, a makeshift shelter for the faculty of arts. Not long thereafter the French, British, and American troops rolled into Freiburg and began the process of rebuilding Germany, setting up a "de-Nazification committee" at the university to discern which of the Freiburg professors were guilty of collaboration. Heidegger's card came up, and he did not fare well. Although he was suspended from teaching and forced into early retirement, his

26. Heidegger's speeches and writings of this period are the strongest witness to his political beliefs. They are published in Richard Wolin, ed., *The Heidegger Controversy: A Critical Reader* (Cambridge: MIT Press, 1993).

collaboration was not deemed grave enough to warrant imprisonment. Through the intervention of Jaspers, Heidegger was given a pension to help him continue his philosophical work. Heidegger had approached Jaspers for a character reference, believing his former friend (with whom he had not spoken in years), whose war record was unblemished by Nazi collaboration, would come to his aid and clear up the mess by telling the committee that Heidegger's involvement with the Nazis was marginal. Jaspers did the opposite. He said that under no circumstances should Heidegger be allowed to continue to teach. He called Heidegger's thinking undemocratic and authoritarian — exactly what the German youth did not need at this tender moment in their history. On the other hand, Jaspers added, Heidegger was one of the most significant thinkers of the century; he must be permitted to write and publish.[27]

Heidegger took the forced retirement badly, suffering a nervous breakdown and retreating into the seclusion of his Black Forest hut. A steady stream of French intellectuals who had been reading Heidegger throughout the war years helped remove the Nazi stain from his reputation by beating a path to his door to talk to him about philosophy. Heidegger was allowed to return to teaching in the 1950s and enjoyed a comeback as a popular lecturer and critic of technology. This period is marked by Heidegger's return to religious questions. No longer concerned with Christian theology, he began to speak in mystical terms of the return of the lost sense of the holy, a forgotten unity of earth, sky, mortals, and divinities. Whatever else we might make of the strange language of the late Heidegger, it shows beyond a doubt that Hans-Georg Gadamer is correct in referring to Heidegger as a fundamentally religious thinker.[28]

However far he may have moved beyond the Catholic piety of his youth and the radical politics of the 1930s, Heidegger never cleanly broke with either Catholicism or Nazism. These narratives of his early life re-

27. Jasper's letter is published in Wolin, *The Heidegger Controversy,* 144-51.

28. Hans-Georg Gadamer, "Being Spirit God," in *Heidegger's Ways,* trans. John W. Stanley (Albany: State University of New York Press, 1994), 182-83: "It was clear to Heidegger that it would be intolerable to speak of God like science speaks about its objects; but what that might mean, to speak of God — this was the question that motivated him and pointed out his way of thinking."

mained "thorns in his side,"[29] tormenting him with a sense of lingering inauthenticity about his lack of courage to either appropriate or break definitively with them. In Germany one must identify one's religious affiliation for tax purposes; on his tax returns Heidegger identified himself as a Catholic to the end of his life. And, as his critics never tire of pointing out, Heidegger never renounced the political views that led him to the Nazi Party and the rectorship of the University of Freiburg. Heidegger's Dasein remained to the end "as it already was."

29. In a letter to Karl Jaspers of 1935 Heidegger describes his relationship to his native religion and the failure of the rectorship as two "thorns in his side." Heidegger, cited in Ott, *Heidegger*, 37.

CHAPTER 2

Phenomenology

Without suggesting that the two can be cleanly separated, in this chapter I consider Heidegger's contribution to phenomenology as distinct from his contributions to ontology. The distinction to be made here is not one of separation: the early Heidegger was a phenomenologist concerned with ontological problems; the later Heidegger understood himself to be an ontologist who had taken a detour through phenomenology. It is indisputable, however, that questions of phenomenological method precede Heidegger's preoccupation with ontology by many years. This of course complicates Heidegger's simplified interpretation of himself as an ontologist from his grammar-school days onward;[1] it also undermines the myth according to which Heidegger is a self-styled genius firmly confining himself to "a single thought that one day stands still like a star in the world's sky."[2]

This chapter is not a summary of *Being and Time*. Dozens of these already exist, and I see no need to write another. Rather, the chapter is a series of ad hoc forays into Heideggerian phenomenology written on the assumption that immersion into the phenomenological conversation is more effective than a linear and systematic introduction.

Heidegger is popularly believed to have decentered reason in a tradition that was entrenched in rationalism since the seventeenth century.

1. Heidegger, "My Way to Phenomenology" (1963).
2. Heidegger, "The Thinker as Poet," in *Poetry, Language, Thought,* trans. Albert Hofstadter (New York: HarperCollins, 2001), 4.

He is commonly understood to have defined reason as something that emerges precisely when something breaks down in the smooth everydayness of Dasein's unthinking being-in-the-world. This simplified picture naturally lacks nuance. Heidegger draws an important distinction between understanding, which is coextensive with human life — fore-theoretical, concrete, and contextual — and knowledge, which is a special activity for particular circumstances (working in a laboratory, writing an exam) — theoretical, abstract, and tending to forget its worldly context. According to Heidegger, Western philosophy from Descartes to Husserl is obsessed with theoretical knowledge to the extent of forgetting or suppressing the understanding natural to life. Phenomenological truth is found not in theory but in a delicate analysis of understanding that resists translating fore-theoretical and contextual thinking into abstract concepts. The work of finding a method adequate to the phenomenological task consumed the first ten years of Heidegger's career. In his first lectures as Husserl's assistant, Heidegger begins to overhaul Husserl's descriptive analysis of the recurring and universal structures of human cognition, transforming the latter's essentialist eidetics into a "formally indicative" account of human living, a project Heidegger calls "the hermeneutics of facticity." This is not intended as counterphenomenology but as a radicalization of Husserl's project. Beside Husserl's famous call "back to the things themselves,"[3] Heidegger writes in the margins of his copy of Husserl's *Logical Investigations:* "[W]e mean to take Husserl at his word!" Husserl's aim is to leave behind the metaphysical and epistemological debates about idealism and realism, mind and body, and to give as true an account as language permits of conscious experience. As Heidegger points out in the introduction to *Being and Time,* "phenomenology" is comprised of two Greek terms, "phenomenon" and "logos." A phenomenon is that which appears, the experienced as such (from the Greek *phainein,* "to show," "to come into the light"); logos means word, reason, or language. Phenomenology, then, is *the language that speaks of that which shows itself.* In Heidegger's own words, phenomenology means "to let that which shows itself be seen

3. Husserl, *Logical Investigations,* trans. J. N. Findlay (New York: Humanities Press, 1970), 252.

from itself in the very way in which it shows itself" (BT, 34). One of the assumptions behind this definition is that scientific talk does not adequately allow that which shows itself to show itself in the way in which it shows itself; scientific discourse is in the habit of distorting the given by cutting it to fit categories that are not native to experience.

Husserl seeks to reestablish philosophy on rigorously scientific terrain by inventing a method for anchoring philosophical analysis in the indisputably given. At the same time, he means to remove all arbitrary restrictions on what can and cannot qualify as an object of philosophical research. For Husserl, if the object is given in any sense, it is a legitimate theme for phenomenology. Husserl's "principle of principles" demands that phenomenology submit itself to the criterion of intuitive presence by accepting and articulating as given whatever is intuitively given — and by doing so within the limits within which the given thing is intuited.[4] Everything that can be intuited is thus a legitimate subject for phenomenological analysis: if something can be intuitively experienced, it can also be described. With this move Husserl displaces the positivism tyrannizing the sciences ("that alone is real which is measurable, i.e., localizable in space and time"). He also places a check on metaphysics and its tendency to extrapolate from the given to a supersensible causal structure. He suspends ("brackets") theories about reality, offering instead a formal account of the conscious life of the human being. For Husserl, philosophy has managed to prove, deduce, and argue for various and many positions, but it has yet to come up with a simple description of the fundamental experiences constituting consciousness. Husserl brackets the so-called big questions — about whether the world is out there, whether God exists, or whether we can know anything — using a method he calls the *epoché* (a Greek word meaning "suspending") — so that we can attend to the original givens of human experience.

Heidegger supports Husserl's removal of rationalistic and positiv-

---

4. Edmund Husserl, *Ideas: General Introduction to Pure Phenomenology,* trans. W. R. Boyce Gibson (New York: Humanities Press, 1976), 1:82: "*[E]very primordial dator Intuition* [an alternative translation is 'originary presentive intuition'] *is a source of authority [rechtsquelle] for knowledge, that whatever presents itself in 'intuition' in primordial form* (as it were in its bodily reality), *is simply to be accepted as it gives itself out to be,* though *only within the limits in which it then presents itself.*"

istic censors that relegate the nonsensible data of consciousness (memories, dreams, emotions) to the status of something less than real. Husserl, however, does not go far enough for Heidegger in the direction of a return to concrete experience: Husserl's emphasis on intuitive presence remains a foothold for the very positivism he hopes to displace. As far as Heidegger is concerned, intuition is only one of a variety of ways of experiencing the world, a specific mode of experience correlative to immediate physical or sensuous presence. If we are to be appropriately faithful to the manifold variety of conscious experiences, we need to relativize intuition and the mode of presence which corresponds with it by elaborating other modes of experience, and above all by resisting the fetish for "presence in the present" as criterion of full phenomenality. Heidegger's restatement of the principle of principles (i.e., his definition of phenomenology) substitutes "showing" for "intuiting." The measure of phenomenality is not found in a fixed subjective mode of apprehension; rather, each phenomenon itself stipulates the means by which it is to be apprehended. The criterion for admittance to phenomenological discourse, then, is for Heidegger the showing of the thing, whatever that involves, and not, as in Husserl's account, the thing's availability to intuition. As Heidegger develops this critique, he becomes aware that it penetrates a core tendency in Western philosophy, of which Husserl himself represents the latest repetition. Western philosophy has always overemphasized the significance of the theoretical attitude for understanding human existence; only under special circumstances, however, are human beings ever "intuitors" of present objects, truly "detached" in their knowing. The theoretical attitude is consolidated by rendering the absolutization of intuition the only legitimate access to phenomena. For Heidegger, we rarely experience this kind of disinterested subjectivity in everyday living. We are for the most part preoccupied with our tasks in the world; far from being detached, we are concerned about things not as knowers but as doers. Husserl's project is not a phenomenology of lived experience; it is yet another phenomenology of knowledge.

Husserl's phenomenology does make significant advances, in Heidegger's opinion, especially insofar as it overcomes the traditional dichotomy between subject and object. Ever since Descartes's cleaving of being into two irreducible poles — subjectivity or thinking and objectivity or extension — philosophy has labored with the skeptical problem of knowledge: How can we know that our thinking accurately reflects objectivity? How can the subject be sure that it reaches the object? Drawing on scholastic psychology, Husserl's teacher Franz Brentano argues that consciousness is never given without an object. Consciousness is not some kind of empty space in the brain, a receptacle of sense impressions from which pictures of objects are formed that may or may not correspond to real things. Consciousness is "intentional," always directed toward something, even if only itself; it is not a thing or a space for things, but an activity, a directedness toward objects. The Cartesian project of trying to bridge the divide between subject and object is therefore a response to a pseudoproblem: Descartes sets up the problem by falsely assuming the existence of the chasm in the first place. The rediscovery of intentionality opens up the possibility of taking note of the different kinds of objects consciousness can intend, and of distinguishing between them on the basis of alternative modes of intending. It is not sufficient to record *what* the object is; the phenomenologist must also discuss *how* consciousness is oriented toward the object. Indeed, the *how* of consciousness makes the object *what* it is. Husserl accordingly distinguishes two sides of every conscious experience: *noēma*, the *what* of consciousness, and *noēsis*, the *how*.

For Heidegger the analysis of intentionality, while going some distance toward correcting Cartesian dualism, remains insufficiently primordial, bound up as it is with the language of subjectivity. Heidegger agrees with Husserl that the proper theme of phenomenology is the given as such (understood in its broadest sense as that which can be experienced). He departs from Husserl in his understanding of the structure and mode of access to the given, and consequently his understanding of the structure of the given itself. Insofar as he renders absolute the theoretical comportment of being, Husserl is deemed by Heidegger to have remained complicit with Western philosophy's forgetfulness of the fore-theoretical ("factical") stratum of living. The subject-object relationship is for Heidegger only one among many ways in which Dasein can be "comported" to the world. The most basic comportments of Dasein cannot be adequately articulated in the language of subject and object, of *noēsis* and *noēma*. Prior to the project of knowledge, Dasein is

immersed in everydayness, lost in practical concerns that are determined by its unthematized preoccupation with its own death. In
everydayness Dasein is disclosed not as a subject-ego, but as a being that
is always outside itself in the temporalizing practical, social, and existential preoccupations that Heidegger refers to as "care" *(Sorge)* or
"being-ahead-of-itself-in-already-being-in-a-world" (BT, 192). On an everyday level Dasein is not a mode of directedness toward objects, but a
"being-in-the-world" absorbed in caring for itself, for the others with
which it always exists, and for the things that surround it.

While Husserl elaborates the varieties of intentions that constitute
the subject-object relation, Heidegger focuses on those dimensions of
experience that elude the theoretical attitude. He asks why the phenomena that are closest to us — life, meaning, time — slip through every concept. The epistemological claim that every knowable thing is an object of
sorts fails to do justice to our everyday way of being with things. The
things around you in the room in which you are reading this are things
that have not yet been thematized, intuited, or objectified, but are nonetheless part of your lived horizon. They are with you and you are with
them in a certain way. They are not objects awaiting the gaze of your subjectivity, and you are not a subject in relation to them. The subject-object
paradigm describes only one particular way of being with things: the way
of being of science, that is, the being of the knowing subject. In "average
everydayness," Heidegger writes in *Being and Time,* things are not intentional objects or "present-at-hand," but "ready-to-hand" (BT, 69). I do not
for the most part engage things as objectively present with objectifiable
attributes or predictable qualities. They are rather the "equipment" of my
life. I simply reach for them when I need them, and in so doing display
my intimate familiarity with how they work. Things can be defined as objects only by being "de-worlded," abstracted from the nest of relations in
which they originally show themselves. The "present-at-hand" is abstract and worldless; the "ready-to-hand" is nested in the contextual
whole of my living. The hammer, which can be objectified as a present-
at-hand object — weighing so much, having a certain shape, and belonging to a class of artifacts — is originally the ready-to-hand tool swinging
in my hand as I build my house: unintuited, nonobjective, and indistinguishable from the referential whole within which such activity is possi-

ble, namely, the world of planning, constructing, and sheltering. A tool is fore-theoretically determined by what it serves to do. As such it cannot be understood apart from the ones to whom it renders service, their purposes, and the other things to which it is related. In contrast to the present-at-hand, the ready-to-hand cannot be thought without the relational whole of factical life *(die Bewandtnisganzheit).* To define a thing I must first lift it out of the world and place it before me as an instance of a class; without its fore-theoretical context I would have no acquaintance with the thing whatsoever.

Perplexed by Husserl's failure to remain true to "the things themselves," Heidegger begins to question why facticity is never properly thematized in philosophy. Facticity seems to have a tendency to avoid or lose itself: something difficult, burdensome, and strenuous about existence thrusts us into a repressive flight from our being-in-the-world. The theoretical attitude is symptomatic of this flight insofar as objective distance allows Dasein to avoid thinking about the ambiguities of factical life. This self-concealing, self-fleeing tendency of Dasein furthermore suggests that phenomenology is only possible as hermeneutics. The hermeneutics of facticity is a phenomenology that proceeds with the assumption that life in all its concreteness and ambiguity does not initially show itself to the philosophical gaze. Whereas phenomenology for Husserl is *theoretical,* a direct elaboration of the structure of experience by means of reflection on conscious acts, phenomenology under Heidegger becomes *hermeneutical,* the provisional thematization of that which cannot be directly accessed through reflection but which must be gestured to indirectly by means of deliberately indeterminate terms. Heidegger calls such terms "formal indications." "Consciousness" does not originally "intuit" things, but rather "understands" them, that is, finds them intelligible, meaningful, and apparent within the horizon of Dasein's practical involvement with them. A thing is not first "given" to us as an intentional object; it is first revealed to us as a historical nexus of meaning. Articulating this fore-theoretical sense of meaning requires a careful use of language. Traditional conceptual language objectifies fore-theoretical experience. Even Husserl's deployment of *noēsis* and *noēma* leaves behind the concrete richness of factical life. Phenomenology must abandon its reliance on univocal language and precise definitions if it is to remain true to its word and describe the given purely as the given gives itself.

This methodological problem was among the first to be analyzed by Heidegger. In his 1915 book on Duns Scotus, he examines how the language of definition always misses the singularity of experience by substituting universals for the *haecceity* of life. Heidegger's early phenomenology retains something of this Scotistic emphasis on the singularity and ineffability of being. The search for a lighter methodological touch, a language tailored to the subject (rather than a subject cut to fit the language), drew Heidegger into areas of research that were not at the time associated with phenomenology. The negative language of medieval mysticism that points the way precisely by leaving the ineffable unnamed; Kierkegaard's method of indirect communication, designed to agitate the individual into self-appropriation by disburdening him of knowledge; and Luther's notion of the crucified emerging as divinity revealed in its opposite form — such are the unlikely sources that play an essential if hidden role in Heidegger's development of a noninvasive phenomenology of facticity.[5]

Heidegger draws on a more mainstream philosophical source in Aristotle's *Nicomachean Ethics,* a text that occupied him for several years in the early 1920s, during which time he taught multiple seminars and lecture courses on Aristotle and even contemplated writing a book on the subject. Aristotle begins his treatise with the disclaimer that ethics can only approximate the certainty achievable in other sciences. Ethics deals with the problems of everyday living, with things that can be otherwise and decisions that must be tailored to unique and unrepeatable situations. One's approach to ethics must befit the subject matter; demonstrative knowledge — *epistēmē* — is possible in metaphysics and mathematics, but the best we can hope for in ethics is to achieve a kind of approximate clarity.[6] There are times when the standard scientific reli-

5. I have analyzed these influences on Heidegger at some length in my *The Early Heidegger and Medieval Philosophy: Phenomenology for the Godforsaken* (Washington, D.C.: Catholic University of America Press, 2006).

6. Aristotle, *Nicomachean Ethics,* trans. W. D. Ross, in *The Basic Works of Aristotle,* ed. Richard McKeon (New York: Random House, 1941), 6.5.1139a33-1140b: "Therefore, since scientific knowledge involves demonstration, but there is no demonstration of things whose

ance upon definitions and precise language must be suspended. When this happens we will at best sketch the matter "roughly and in outline," leaving room for revision and the eventual understanding that comes only with diligent application.[7] Heidegger finds in Aristotle's ethics a philosophy that stays with the flux and temporality of human living instead of merely abstracting from it. For Aristotle, ethical knowledge is the product of *phronēsis,* or practical wisdom; it cannot be abstracted from the situation. One can "know" virtue only by doing it, which is why one cannot teach ethics as a theoretical discipline. Ethics, Aristotle continues, can be taught only by example: the student must learn, through trial and error and the messy business of living, to imitate the ethical person until virtue, the capacity to choose the mean between hedonism and self-denial in any given situation, becomes second nature.

In Heidegger's view, strict definitions and technical terms (the meanings of which are unvarying from one application to the next) are as inappropriate to phenomenology as Aristotle understands them to be to ethics. Husserl's ideal of "apodicticity," a definitive and binding account, is a mathematical criterion unsuitable to the careful description of life. Like poetry, which stays close to the world by leaving everything as it is, phenomenology must find noninvasive uses of language that let things show themselves in themselves. The young Heidegger's method of formal indication entails the search for a language that gestures rather than defines. It is a deliberately open-ended use of terms that are insufficient until they have been completed or "enacted" by the addressee. Formally indicative phenomenology can be genuinely understood only by being applied; moreover, every application restructures the meaning of the term in a unique and incommunicable way. Heidegger calls us to *live through* rather than theoretically inspect phenomena. On a superfi-

---

first principles are variable (for all such things might actually be otherwise), and since it is impossible to deliberate about things that are of necessity, practical wisdom cannot be scientific knowledge."

7. Aristotle, *Ethics* 1.3.1094b19-28: "We must be content, then, in speaking of such subjects and with such premises to indicate the truth roughly and in outline. . . . In the same spirit, therefore, should each type of statement be *received;* for it is the mark of an educated man to look for precision in each class of things just so far as the nature of the subject admits."

cial reading, *Being and Time* is a catalogue of terms coined to character-ize human existence: "thrownness," "fallenness," "care," "attunement," "understanding," etc. New readers will do well to note that Heidegger never offers definitions of these terms. The language is left strategically undetermined. His model is too indefinite to be considered abstractly; it demands application.

At the same time that he formally indicates the factic, Heidegger takes a turn toward a neo-Kantian style of transcendental methodology. The tension between transcendental and factical philosophy in *Being and Time* is never adequately resolved by Heidegger; ultimately it precip-itates the conflict between the ontological and the ontic that threatens to overturn the entire enterprise in division 2. Heidegger cannot stay on the transcendental/ontological/existential level but must return at key moments to the ontic/existentiell level to find a clue for how to proceed. *Being and Time* begins with an examination of "the conditions of the pos-sibility" of "the question of the meaning of being." As we saw in the previ-ous chapter, "the transcendental" is not, as it sounds, something other-worldly or supernatural; quite the contrary. It concerns the hidden conditions that make a given experience possible. The transcendental never properly shows itself — it is not a phenomenon in the strict literal sense. It is rather that which must operate *behind* the showing in order for phenomena to show themselves as they in fact do. "Horizon" is a fa-vorite metaphor of transcendental philosophy. A horizon is never objectified; and yet no object is without its horizon. Heidegger is search-ing for the conditions of the possibility of experiencing the questionabil-ity of being, the horizon of the understanding of being. For this reason he begins with an analysis of the human being. Dasein has an "ontic prior-ity." Among all the things that are (the ontic order), this one being in par-ticular, Dasein, constitutes the way of entry into ontology (the deep structure of the ontic) to the extent that it is the only being for whom be-ing is an issue. Only Dasein betrays a "preunderstanding" of being that may be taken as the starting point of analysis. Dasein is the being that asks the question of being. To ask this question, Heidegger tells us, it must have some glimmer of what it is looking for.

"The Dasein analytic" (division 1 of part 1 of *Being and Time*) is by far the most famous thing Heidegger ever wrote. It is an analysis of the being of the human being interpreted not as a thing or a subject but as "being-in-the-world." New readers are immediately struck by the peculiar language Heidegger employs to express insights that he insists are not possible with the old lexicon. *Dasein* is a German word used to connote the existence of anything — the *Dasein* of a chair, for example, or the *Dasein* of a cup of coffee. Heidegger's unusual deployment of the word as a noun confronts the German reader with the etymological structure of the word: *da* is German for "there"; *Sein* is German for "being." Where philosophy traditionally speaks in terms of immaterial substances — of "soul" or "subjectivity" — Heidegger speaks of "being-there." In the wake of Heidegger we can no longer take for granted the terms of worldless subjectivity, timeless soul, or substantial personal identity. Dasein is a being that is always there. It is temporal by definition, and never without the world. The modern problematic of "the reality of the external world" is a chimera generated by the notion of timeless and worldless subjectivity. The term "subject" is so loaded with philosophical baggage that it cannot be used without summoning up philosophical ghosts: the problem of the external world, the question of solipsism, or the craving for certainty.

One cannot understand *Being and Time* without first grappling with Heidegger's distinction — so tersely and inadequately articulated, and ultimately, in my view, untenable — between an "existential" analysis of human life and an "existentiell" reflection on how to live. The "existential" is ontological in the strict sense: it concerns the being of the human being in a formal sense rather than in any concrete, particular historical, ethical, political, or theological context; existence in abstraction from any particular individual's existence. "Existentiell" refers to what is popularly considered an "existential" consideration, namely, a first-person reflection on "the meaning of life" in a broadly ethical sense and with a view to deciding how best to live. Careful readers of this book may feel the urge to say: Wait a minute — isn't it Heidegger's point that a philosophy of the human being cannot be done in the abstract and theoretical register but must be concrete, applied, and lived? Yes, and here is where difficulties emerge: Heidegger wishes to be both "formal" and "applied"; he wishes to discuss structures that make no sense in abstraction, but without abandoning altogether the phenomenological project of describing rather than prescribing. One can, I hope, see how the problem of formal indication remains the central issue for *Being and Time:* like Aristotle, who cannot write a science of ethics because ethics is understood only in application (it can be learned only by experience) and yet who must say something, however roughly and provisionally, by way of outlining the contours of the discussion, which must be filled out by the ethically choosing individual, Heidegger finds himself at the extreme limit of theory. Nothing is more distinctive of being human than existentiell reflection; it shows that Dasein is a being for whom being is always an issue. However, Heidegger does not understand his contribution to pertain primarily to "existentiell" reflection; he is ostensibly not offering wisdom to live by. And yet he cannot remain altogether indifferent to existentiell considerations because ontology must take its lead from the ontic:

> Dasein always understands itself in terms of its existence — in terms of a possibility of itself: to be itself or not itself. Dasein has either chosen these possibilities itself, or got itself into them, or grown up in them already. Only the particular Dasein decides its existence, whether it does so by taking hold or by neglecting. The question of existence never gets straightened out except through existing itself. The understanding of oneself which leads along this way we call "existentiell." The question of existence is one of Dasein's ontical "affairs." This does not require that the ontological structure of existence should be theoretically transparent. The question about that structure aims at the analysis of what constitutes existence. The context of such structures we call "existentiality." Its analytic has the character of an understanding which is not existentiell, but rather *existential.* (BT, 12)

An existentiell reflection is highly individual, my activity of seeking self-understanding, discerning how I should act in a particular situation, which will necessarily differ from how others understand themselves and how others ground their actions. An existential analysis, by contrast, concerns not me in my particular ethical/spiritual predicament, but my mode of being-in-the-world in a formal sense, which therefore applies to all. When I do ontology I suspend the personal historical context of my existence for the sake of a more general, formal understanding of living.

Existentiell thinking need not be existential; churches, for example, are full of authentic believers who have no notion of ontology, nor any interest therein. On the other hand, Heidegger says, ontology cannot be equally indifferent to existentiell considerations. At a crucial point in *Being and Time* and with the purpose of fleshing out his analysis of existence, Heidegger returns to an existentiell ideal of a genuinely human life. Indeed, one cannot discuss existence, it seems, without staking a claim about how it is best for Dasein to be: "But the roots of the existential analytic, on its part, are ultimately *existentiell,* that is, *ontical.* Only if the inquiry of philosophical research is itself seized upon in an existentiell manner as a possibility of the Being of each existing Dasein, does it become at all possible to disclose the existentiality of existence and to undertake an adequately founded ontological problematic" (BT, 13). This, in my view, is among the most inscrutable passages written by Heidegger. What does it mean? Are we to understand that philosophy is here regarded as an existentiell ideal in itself with a claim to total commitment equal to or exceeding other ways of life? If that is the case, what has happened to the ontological/ontic distinction? Or are we to understand that an existential-ontological treatment of Dasein without recourse to an existentiell commitment, as a clue or indicator of Dasein's hidden depths, is not possible? If this is the right interpretation (and it must be this, for otherwise the ontological/ontic distinction collapses), on what grounds can philosophy decide which among the many possible existentiell ideals is to guide ontology since from the outset, philosophy has declared a neutrality with respect to existentiell commitments? The ideal of Christian charity and the ideal of atheistic hedonism are both existentiell or ontic beliefs prescribing vastly different ways of living. On what grounds is ontology to choose between the two? How could it prefer one ideal over the other if the grounds for preference are not ontological but ontic? But if it cannot choose, then how is it to continue with its ontology?

The first *existential* claim to be made is that Dasein is being-in-the-world. By "world" Heidegger means something other than the universe or the totality of things that are: world cannot be without Dasein. When Descartes endeavors to empty his mind of the world and to select from his experiences only those phenomena about which he feels indubitably certain, he fails to realize that he has not left the world at all: the world remains what he continues to think about. The subject cannot cut itself out of the world and then reestablish relations with it. In one of his earliest sketches of the hermeneutics of facticity, Heidegger discusses human existence in terms of three different modes of being-in-the-world: "the surrounding world," "the world of the self," and the "with-world" (GA58, 43-46). Each of these modes of being-in-the-world is constitutive of human existence; to be is to be "in" an environment, to be a self, and to be with others. The first of these modes designates the context of things, locales, and events that make up a life. The second includes the psychological, emotional, and historical phenomena of "inner" life. The third mode refers to family, culture, and society. Like a formal distinction in Duns Scotus, the three worlds are inseparable sides of the same phenomenon. One can look at the world in three ways, namely, as the world around us, as the world within us, and as the world between us. At no point, however, can we pull the world out of Dasein or Dasein out of the world. World is the referential whole *(Bewandtnisganzheit)* of Dasein's existence, the always already understood context of everyday living that makes possible the variety of ways of experiencing things. Things are handy or useful only in the context of a world. A thing has its being in a set of relationships that ultimately refer to Dasein and its projects; apart from Dasein, there are no things. In a polemic with Husserl disguised as a critique of Descartes, Heidegger contrasts his notion of world with the Cartesian concept of world as the "extended thing" *(res extensa)* distinguishable from the "thinking thing" *(res cogitans)* (BT, 95). Descartes's concept of world, like Husserl's intentional object, privileges one particular way of being-in-the-world over all others: *epistēmē* or *intellectus* — the mode of being predicated on accessing other beings as knowledge.

Descartes's aim is certainty. He privileges mathematical knowledge as the only genuine way of apprehending things. The being that is grasped by such knowledge has, for Descartes, an unchanging presence: it "constantly remains." The ideal of constant presence is not unique to Descartes; it has been the ontological ideal of the Western tradition since Plato. Philosophy after Descartes becomes more adept at figuring beings as constant presence. Heidegger's question to Descartes — and Husserl — is as simple as it is original. Granted that experience is change, flux, mutability, and event, emergence and withdrawal from presence: Why is presence privileged over absence?

Being and Time has no theory of knowledge. Heidegger endeavors to think phenomena prior to their transposition into the order of knowledge. To bring about this return to a more primordial way of philosophizing, Heidegger retrieves the ancient Greek word for truth, *alētheia*, interpreting it literally as "unconcealment." Heidegger argues that before truth came to mean the correspondence between an idea in my mind and a thing in the world, it was the "self-showing," the unconcealment, of things. Unconcealment is a complex thought. Two ideas are at work in it, namely, the notion of hiddenness or concealment on the one hand, and its negation or unconcealment on the other. For Heidegger, things come to appear in the light of their unconcealment, which means that they are not always standing in this light. Primordial truth is the experience of something *coming* into the light; the opposite of this kind of truth is not falsehood but noncognizance. Heidegger's point here is that it is nonsensical to speak of falsehood on the level of primordial truth. Everything that shows itself is true insofar as it shows itself. Falsehood becomes relevant only at a metalevel at which propositions are used to describe what has already been shown. Only at this secondary level we observe a correspondence to fact; our propositions accurately point out what has already been shown. Here the possibility of falsehood arises, the possibility of a statement that does not point out what has been shown but covers it over again. Heidegger claims that the elevation of judgment over unconcealment has resulted in a forgetfulness of primordial truth, which is not a correspondence but "letting something be seen."

It is curious that the Dasein analytic begins with an analysis of tools and things of use. Tools are apparently closer to us than other persons in the context of average everydayness. Others are there, but only mediately through the referentiality of tools. My hammer is for constructing my house; my house is for sheltering my family. The referential totality that is the world includes the existence of other Dasein as those for the sake of whom certain things are done. We shall say more about Heidegger's subordination of human relations to ontology in a later chapter. It is not that Heidegger is an individualist. Quite the contrary.

When we speak of the being of the human-being, we speak always of a being-with-others. Dasein does not need empathy to believe that there are proximate others possessing a way of being analogous to its own. Dasein is always already with others. Indeed, for the most part Dasein lives its life through others, in the sense that Dasein's being has been taken from it by others. Average everyday Dasein sees things as others see them; it judges as others judge. It lives its life carried along by the cares and values of its community. Heidegger's notion of being-with overturns modern subjectivism and reconfigures Western anthropology, which assumes the "incommunicability" of the "immaterial soul" or, in a modern idiom, the privacy of subjectivity. Dasein is not a self-possessed subject who enters into reciprocal relations with other equally self-possessed subjects; Dasein exists for the most part in an undifferentiated herdlike submersion in the collective "they" *(Das Mann)*. "Initially and for the most part," I am not a subject in ethical-political relation with others. Rather, I am not yet an "I" at all. My "I" is the collective ego of the community. Like Luther's fallen man, so sunk into self-oblivious ways of thinking and behaving that it no can longer be said to possess a self, Heidegger's Dasein is originally undifferentiated from the faceless mass of men and women who have not yet chosen their destiny. Dasein is not originally individuated. It must achieve individuation.

To be colonized by others is to live "inauthentically." Others are not persons at the level of the they-self. The they is an undifferentiated collective that encourages me to avoid the burden of being myself. Authenticity consists in emancipating oneself from this faceless mass, standing apart, and living out of one's own proper convictions and insights. Somehow we are to avoid hearing this in an evaluative sense: authenticity is not better or more praiseworthy than inauthenticity. To be in the world as not-ourselves, *un-eigentlich* — literally, "not-my-own-ness" — is neither sinful nor evil. Dasein is originally lost, submerged in the superficialities of social life: inauthenticity has primacy over authenticity. If it happens at all, authenticity is an achievement and a modification of Dasein's habitual way of being. This logical reversal of the relation of the negative to the positive is essential to Heidegger's thinking: the negative, which seems to be founded, i.e., presupposing the positive, is actually the more primordial and founding structure. Just as possibility is higher than actuality (BT, 38) and absence is older than presence, inauthenticity is for Heidegger more basic than authenticity.

Heidegger sets up a situation of crisis by assuming a deep distrust of social relations. Dasein is occupied territory, under the tyranny of a mediocre majority hostile to everything unique and exceptional: "In this averageness with which it prescribes what can and may be ventured, it keeps watch over everything exceptional that thrusts itself to the fore" (BT, 127). This majority polices Dasein, enforcing its prohibition on uniqueness by the threat of ostracization. He who stands out risks friendlessness. Since truth for Heidegger is always a surprise, a break with the status quo — an unveiling — it is vigorously outlawed by the they. In fact, nothing is sacred for the they, which quashes the aristocratic claims of truth and inoculates knowledge by reducing it to an empty slogan. They cannot ever be surprised: "Overnight, everything that is primordial gets glossed over as something that has been well known. Everything gained by struggle becomes just something to be manipulated. Every secret loses its force. This care of averageness reveals in turn an essential tendency of Dasein which we call the leveling down of all possibilities of Being" (BT, 127). Falsehood becomes a way of life protected by custom if not by law. Anyone who distinguishes herself from the herd can expect vilification. "Every kind of priority gets noiselessly suppressed" (BT, 127). You do not belong to yourself. Everything you say and do merely entrenches "their" power.

> In utilizing public means of transport and in making use of information services such as the newspaper, every other is like the next. This being-with-one-another dissolves one's own Dasein completely into the kind of Being of "the others," in such a way, indeed, that the others, as distinguishable and explicit, vanish more and more. In this inconspicuousness and unascertainability, the real dictatorship of the "they" is unfolded. We take pleasure and enjoy ourselves as they take pleasure. We read, see, and judge about literature and art as they see and judge; likewise we shrink back from the "great mass" as they shrink back; we find shocking what they find shocking. The "they," which is nothing definite, and which all are, though not as the sum, prescribes the kind of being of everydayness. (BT, 126-27)

Heidegger makes free use of ethical-theological terms throughout *Being and Time,* for example, "fallenness," "conscience," "guilt," and "temptation," insisting that such terms should not be understood according to either their ethical or their theological senses. Heidegger's notes are full of references to Augustine, Thomas Aquinas, Luther, and Calvin; he insists nonetheless that his terms are not originally theological, and that theologians who use them simply do not understand the deeper ontological ground of their own language. Heidegger presumably clears the way for such primordial understanding by using the terms to gesture formally to an ontological structure that had never before been thematized. I shall have occasion to question Heidegger's assumptions about his own radicality later on. Let us look at one of these theological revisions. "Conscience" appeals to Dasein in the midst of the latter's social stupor, condemning Dasein's fallen state of being, reminding Dasein of its "guilt," its failure to appropriate what is most its own. Dasein is "tempted" to enter into a conspiratorial agreement with the they to maintain the noise necessary to muffle conscience's call. Dasein attests to its "authentic potentiality-for-being" in the face of its conscience, which says nothing even as it casts a disapproving eye on Dasein's everyday inauthenticity ("the call discourses in the uncanny mode of keeping silent" [BT, 277]). If average everydayness were the end of the story, Dasein would remain an incompletely understood phenomenon. Phenomenology must be able to say something about Dasein's potentials for wholeness and self-appropriation if it is to speak credibly about Dasein's fragmented lostness in the they. Who does Dasein become when it chooses itself? How is phenomenology to answer this question if it remains confined to an analysis of Dasein in average everydayness? And yet if phenomenology leaves this safe zone of fallenness (where presumably there is no risk of existentiell commitment), what is to guide it? Heidegger believes that his excursion into the ontic, his selection of an existentiell ideal of living, is phenomenologically justified insofar as the ideal appears, negatively indicated, as it were, in conscience. Authenticity, the existentiell modification of being-in-the-world that restores Dasein to itself, makes its appearance in the fallen order (where phenomenology grounds its analysis) as "the call of conscience": at this depth of phenomenological experience the distinction between the ontological and the ontic breaks down. "The call of conscience has the character of an appeal to Dasein by calling it to its ownmost potentiality-for-Being-its-Self; and this is done by way of *summoning* it to its ownmost Being-guilty" (BT, 269). Conscience, in Heidegger's primordial sense of the term, does not presume any particular religious or ethical training: it is Dasein's native sense of self-accountability, which no amount of inauthentic living can entirely destroy. "The appeal [of conscience] calls back by calling forth: it calls Dasein *forth* to the possibility of taking over, in existing, even that thrown entity which it is; it calls Dasein *back* to its thrownness so as to understand this thrownness as the null basis which it has to take up into existence" (BT, 287). What conscience summons us to is not some true selfhood, hidden like the gold under the dross of everyday social existence. It wordlessly demands, rather, that we appropriate our lack of selfhood. It shows us up as a "null basis," a lack of actuality — an always outstanding project.

The word "authenticity" is best understood through an etymology of the German, *eigentlichkeit.* The root is *eigen,* which means "own." To be authentic is to own oneself. Insofar as the self for Heidegger is primarily futural, owning oneself entails owning one's nonactuality. Ultimately it means owning one's being-unto-death. Authenticity is an existentiell modification of Dasein's relation to itself and others. Heidegger is forced to make an excursus into the ontic, the order of historical enactment of Dasein's potentialities, to complete his ontology; he cannot understand Dasein as whole without first explicating the ontic or existentiell ideal that appeals to Dasein. This comes as somewhat of a surprise. At the outset of the book we are told that a treatise on ontology must resist the temptation to think Dasein in ontic terms, in terms applicable either to things or to particular ways of being-in-the-world. It is on these grounds that Heidegger excludes both natural scientific and religious contributions to existential anthropology. He resists science insofar as it approaches the human being as a thing or an object; he eschews religion insofar as it narrates a specific and historical enactment of human being-in-the-world. And yet, at the decisive moment in the analysis, we discover that ontology is not indifferent to the ontic; not all existentiell ideals are equal, it seems. One in particular, and one alone, can illuminate the whole of Dasein's being. Authenticity is a *possibility* for being-in-the-world; it is not a necessity. One cannot be in the world without one of the three modifications of care: inauthenticity, indifference, or authenticity. Of these modifications, Heidegger tells us, Dasein is typically in a state of inauthenticity. And yet phenomenological ontology cannot stay with the average and everyday experience of Dasein; the shadow cast by conscience directs ontology, as it does the individual Dasein, away from the they back toward Dasein's ownmost possibility for being.

Inauthenticity is at root a flight from death, driven internally by an undercurrent of anxiety about Dasein's end that suffuses all of human living. The significance of death occupies the better part of division 2 of *Being and Time.* Death is Dasein's "ownmost possibility — non-relational, certain and as such indefinite, not to be outstripped" (BT, 258-59). Death is Dasein's ownmost possibility: here the comaraderie of the they reaches its limit. Death is nonrelational: no one can die in my place. It is certain: there can be no doubt that death is Dasein's end. It is not to be outstripped: no amount of avoidance or denial will ultimately succeed in delivering Dasein from the burden of living toward its death. As my ownmost possibility, death is constitutive of my life; to own it is to authenticate my existence, to be myself.

> The non-relational character of death, as understood in anticipation, individualizes Dasein down to itself. It makes manifest that all Being-alongside the things with which we concern ourselves, and all Being-with Others, will fail us when our ownmost potentiality-for-Being is at issue. . . . Dasein is authentically itself only to the extent that *as* concernful Being-alongside and solicitous Being-with, it projects itself upon its ownmost potentiality-for-Being rather than upon the possibility of the they-self. The entity which anticipates its non-relational possibility, is thus forced by that very anticipation into the possibility of taking over from itself its ownmost Being, and doing so of its own accord. (BT, 263)

In living resolutely unto death, Dasein lifts itself out of the they and becomes itself, if only for a moment that is destined to be swallowed up in fallen everydayness. Death is the essence of Dasein's existence, regardless of whether it appropriates it or not. When it resolutely anticipates death, Dasein becomes transparent to itself, unrepressed and open-eyed about its limitations and future. All Dasein's activities and concerns revolve around this vanishing point. Death is the unthinkable and inevitable truth of human living. Everything we do, say, and think is a reaction to our repressed anxiety in the face of the singularity and isolation of death. It is death and death alone that individuates. Death pulls me out of the collective delirium, giving the lie to my various strategies for mitigating the solitude of existence. Death is the moment when the incommunicable singularity of being-in-the-world comes crashing down on Dasein. If I have lived under the illusion that others carry my being for me, death comes as the shock of that which most intimately concerns me. In death I am entirely alone. When I anticipate my death, I become resolute about my life — all my decisions and actions become enlivened as "my own." Note the paradox here: the future moment that makes me most myself is the moment when I cease to exist.

Heidegger draws a crucial distinction between anticipating *(vorgreifen/vorlaufen)* and expecting *(erwarten)* death. Expecting is awaiting an actualization of a possibility: I expect a train or a promotion. Expectation looks toward realizations of possibilities for being-in-the-world. Death cannot be expected since it is not an actualization or a realization of a way of being-in-the-world. Death is the annulling of all possibility and actuality, the end of all being-in-the-world. We are not to *expect* death, but to *anticipate* it, to live toward it as the nullity that annuls every expectation. To anticipate is to project oneself upon a possibility in such a way as to change one's way of being in time. The student who anticipates one day being a professor of philosophy pursues her studies with resolve and intensity. Whether or not she becomes a professor of philosophy changes nothing with regard to how the anticipation affects her existence. What makes the anticipation of death unique is the nature of death itself as the end of all possibilities for being-in-the-world. In anticipating death I anticipate the negation of my Dasein. Death is the point on the horizon toward which I am always moving but at which I never arrive, for when I do I am not. *"The closest closeness which one may have in Being towards death as a possibility, is as far as possible from anything actual.* The more unveiledly this possibility gets understood, the more purely does the understanding penetrate into it *as the possibility of the impossibility of any existence at all"* (BT, 262). Being-unto-death lives toward death, not calculating the day and the hour, predicting the moment so as to make necessary arrangements, but resolutely making death the meaning of life. To anticipate death is to will possibility over actuality. Since Dasein is nothing other than possibility, a being whose existence is "to be" (in the futural sense), the anticipation of death is a willing of oneself as journey without destination, a being-toward-possibility without the closure of actuality. "Being-towards-death is the anticipation of a potentiality-for-Being of that entity whose kind of Being is anticipation itself" (BT, 262). Living toward death is owning oneself as an unanswerable question.

A major influence on the early Heidegger's phenomenology of death (largely unacknowledged by Heidegger) is the nineteenth-century Danish religious thinker Søren Kierkegaard, for whom anxiety is also characteristic of existence. Kierkegaard distinguishes between anxiety and fear by noting that while fear has an object — I am afraid that I may have cancer, or that thieves may break into my house while I am away — anxiety is object-less.[8] I am not anxious over any one thing in particular, but about everything — which is the same as being anxious about nothing. Anxiety is more characteristic of spirit than happiness. For Kierkegaard, the human being thrives in situations of uncertainty, which is why faith is so appropriate to existence. Subjective interiority blossoms in objective uncertainty: we are never more human than when we risk our lives for a belief invested with infinite significance, in the face of an abyss of inwardness offering no guarantee that the risk will have been worth taking in the end. Inhuman is the life comprised of rational decisions made solely on the basis of certain knowledge. Scientific objectivity tells us nothing about what it means to be human, even as philosophy's most important questions revolve around existence. "Subjectivity, inwardness is truth," declares one of Kierkegaard's pseudonyms.[9] Moreover, subjec-

8. Søren Kierkegaard, *The Concept of Anxiety*, ed. and trans. Reidar Thomte in collaboration with Albert B. Anderson (Princeton: Princeton University Press, 1980), 43.

9. Søren Kierkegaard, *Concluding Unscientific Postscript to* Philosophical Fragments, ed. and trans. Howard V. Hong and Edna H. Hong (Princeton: Princeton University Press, 1992), 207. Kierkegaard ventures a similar argument to Heidegger regarding the necessity of consulting an existentiell ideal in order to fully understand human existence. Faith is

tivity is no more directly communicable than it is scientifically available. The subject must shoulder the burden of existence on a lonely journey without the consolation of objective knowledge or the solace of communal fellowship.

Heidegger takes up the Kierkegaardian theme of the philosophical significance of anxiety in division 1 of *Being and Time.* Anxiety is the affective or emotional manifestation of Dasein's implicit understanding of being-unto-death. Anxiety is not a fear of any one thing, but a more general unease with one's being. Dasein has anxiety in the face of being-in-the-world as such. The context of Heidegger's analysis of anxiety in *Being and Time* is his elaboration of the existential of *Befindlichkeit,* translated variously (and equally unhappily) as "attunement" or "state of mind" (BT, §29). *Befindlichkeit,* from *finden,* "to find," connotes a feeling that is lost in both translations. *Befindlichkeit* is the quality of finding oneself in a certain emotive disposition for reasons that remain obscure. Heidegger's claim that moods and "irrational" emotional states are disclosive of being shows how definitely he breaks with Cartesianism, which seeks to subdue the passions under the aegis of reason. Moods are of utmost significance to Heidegger because they do not lie. Anxiety overtakes us in unguarded moments, compensating for our inauthentic absorption in the world, reminding us that full actuality always eludes Dasein.

Heidegger pursues the theme of anxiety in his 1929 "What Is Metaphysics?" Boredom, being in love, and joy disclose being in important ways, but the pride of place goes to anxiety. "What Is Metaphysics?" begins with an analysis of the question, as old as metaphysics itself, "Why is there something rather than nothing?" If we are able to ask about the

---

philosophically elaborated by Kierkegaard's philosophical pseudonym, Johannes Climacus, not because it is objectively true (it is objectively uncertain) but because it intensifies subjectivity to a maximal degree. Philosophy cannot decide if there is or if there is not a God; but it can note that faith in God maximizes "inwardness." Kierkegaard's superiority over Heidegger consists in the fact that his argument is presented by a pseudonym; it is deflected. Kierkegaard refuses to own the argument. Climacus is comical in his impossible effort to maintain speculative impartiality, his fascination with a life that can only be understood through commitment and his simultaneous refusal to give assent to any one belief about life. Of course, if faith alone maximizes inwardness, subjectivity itself has testified to the truth it seeks, and the philosophical pseudonym must give way to Anti-Climacus, Kierkegaard's Christian pseudonym.

nothing in this question, Heidegger argues in his characteristically para-doxical fashion (as though the question were not primarily about the something, but about the nothing), we must already know about it. When and where do we experience the nothing? If our everyday thinking is pre-occupied with beings, where is the original experience of the nothing lo-cated? To find a clue to an answer, Heidegger offers a functional defini-tion of the nothing as the negation of the totality of beings. When do we experience the totality of beings? Totality is never really available, at least not in an objective or scientific sense. Dasein finds itself thrown into be-ings as a whole: Dasein feels and anticipates totality, but it cannot thematize totality because it stands in the very center of it. A comprehen-sive grasp of the whole is simply not possible. Totality can be felt in cer-tain moods, however: in boredom, joy, and love, according to Heidegger, we sense the whole. Boredom reveals the totality of beings as indifferent, as no longer engaging us. Heidegger does not offer an analogous descrip-tion of the ways in which joy and love bring the whole into view, which is unfortunate — one imagines a very different phenomenology ensuing from love as disclosive of being. Anxiety, for Heidegger, runs deeper in the mystery of existence than either boredom or joy. It is neither fleeting nor occasional; it is pervasive in human life but is rarely acknowledged as such. Repeating the Kierkegaardian insight into the distinction between anxiety and fear, Heidegger gives one of the most compelling descriptions of a human experience in the whole of his early phenomenological works. Anxiety, he tells us, is the experience of feeling the world (so compulsively absorbing in its average everydayness) lose its hold, sink into indiffer-ence, relinquish its place to nothing.

> [A] peculiar calm pervades it. Anxiety is indeed anxiety in the face of . . . , but not in the face of this or that thing. Anxiety in the face of . . . is always anxiety for . . . , but not for this or that. The indeterminate-ness of that in the face of which and for which we become anxious is no mere lack of determination but rather the essential impossibility of determining it. In a familiar phrase this indeterminateness comes to the fore. In anxiety, we say, "one feels ill at ease [*es ist einem unheimlich*]." What is "it" that makes "one" feel ill at ease? We cannot say what it is before which one feels ill at ease. As a whole it is so for

one. All things and we ourselves sink into indifference. This, however, not in the sense of mere disappearance. Rather, in this very receding things turn toward us. The receding of beings as a whole that closes in on us in anxiety oppresses us. We can get no hold on things. In the slipping away of beings only this "no hold on things" comes over us and remains. Anxiety reveals the nothing. We "hover" in anxiety. More precisely, anxiety leaves us hanging because it induces the slipping away of beings as a whole. (WM, 101)

Boredom is a symptom of anxiety: we are waiting for something to emerge and divert our attention again. Anxiety realizes that there is nothing, nothing at all, that will ultimately relieve us of the burden of our being. A peculiar calm pervades it, Heidegger says. We find it strangely quieting to know that nothing works, nothing will do, nothing will last, nothing will satisfy. The experience of the nothing is not the effect of the nothing drawing us toward it. We are not attracted to the nothing; on the contrary, the nothing repels us. At the moment it recoils from the nothing, Dasein experiences the parting gesture of the whole. The totality of beings pulls away from Dasein, revealing the nothing to be the horizon of the whole. The strangeness of everything suddenly colors all experience. Things appear in their sheer contingency, profiled sharply against the abyss. Anxiety is thus indistinguishable from a kind of radical amazement, a feeling of wonder that anything at all should be. Heidegger's point is that the original metaphysical "Why is there something rather than nothing?" arises out of anxiety. We feel that it is strange that things should be, strange that we *are,* rather than not. According to Heidegger, this strangeness is the fuel that fires Greek philosophy. Experience as such, so simple and profound, has been covered over by the history of metaphysics. On the basis of this analysis Heidegger gives us a fresh definition of Dasein as "being held out into the nothing." This is in fact a new definition of transcendence. Where transcendence once meant being-toward-God, the absolute, the good, Heidegger redefines it in an atheistic key. Heidegger argues as early as 1922 that philosophy must be atheistic on principle, not out of obligation to any irreligious creed, but insofar as philosophy's methodology, committed as it is to the finitude of existence, turns away from eternity (PIA, 121 n. 9).

Great courage is required of those who would remain with the nothing that is disclosed in anxiety. Dasein's spontaneous reaction to the nothing is to fill the void with something, to banish the silence with diversions and chatter. We are not all equal in this regard; some of us have resolve enough to stay with the nothing. Here we glimpse Heidegger's notorious elitism, an ample taste of which may be found in his writing of the early 1930s. "Anxiety is usually repressed. Anxiety is there. It is only sleeping. Its breath quivers perpetually through Dasein, only slightly in those who are jittery, imperceptibly in the 'Oh, yes' and the 'Oh, no' of men of affairs; but most readily in the reserved, and most assuredly in those who are basically daring. But those daring ones are sustained by that on which they expend themselves — in order thus to preserve the ultimate grandeur of existence" (WM, 106).

This sounds tragic, but Heidegger insists it is not, going so far as to speak of a "joy" that comes with the anxious anticipation of death (BT, 310). Resolute anticipation is freedom. Heidegger does not believe in free will in any conventional sense. But he does believe in a higher freedom, a freedom that has marked similarities to the freedom of which Spinoza and Schelling speak, namely, that of appropriated necessity. "When by anticipation, one becomes free *for* one's own death, one is liberated . . . in such a way that for the first time one can authentically understand and choose among the factual possibilities lying ahead of that possibility which is not to be outstripped" (BT, 263). The anticipation of death plays a salvific role in Heidegger's economy of Godforsaken existence, the closest thing to a religious experience in *Being and Time*. Death in the work of Heidegger can be likened to the "x" that is filled out by various religious images, for example, Christ in the Western tradition and the Buddha in the Eastern tradition: it is a formal structure, the end of Dasein (end both as goal and cessation), which has been concretely symbolized in historical religious doctrines. Heidegger tries hard to avoid slipping into religion in *Being and Time*, but he cannot help but wax inspirational over the change that anticipation of death effects on Dasein. Death is a revelation of the truth about life: only by anticipating death does Dasein awaken to its fallenness and inauthenticity. Death rescues Dasein from the typically servile and by turns tyrannical inauthenticity that characterizes its relations with others: only in anticipating death can Dasein establish mutually respectful relations to other Dasein. Death brings Dasein back to time. Anticipating death means genuinely understanding that the meaning of being is time. By living toward death Dasein gives itself over wholly to facticity and lives fully in history. *"Anticipation reveals to Dasein its lostness in the they-self, and brings it face to face with the possibility of being itself, primarily unsupported by concernfull solicitude, but of being itself, rather, in an impassioned* **freedom towards death** — *a freedom which has been released from the Illusions of the 'they,' and which is factical, certain of itself, and anxious"* (BT, 266).

This is the *satori* of *Being and Time*, Heidegger's promise of sudden enlightenment: the achievement of "resolute anticipation," which, having accepted finitude, affirms the inherent emptiness of being-in-the-world and says yes to being-unto-death. "Anticipation discloses to existence that its uttermost possibility lies in giving itself up, and thus it shatters all one's tenaciousness to whatever existence one has reached" (BT, 264). As rare as it is precious, anticipation brings us into the present moment for the first time. Our average and everyday preoccupations disperse us in anxious cares and endless projects; anticipation lends to life an energy and focus that are the antithesis of being lost in "the common-sense ambiguity of that publicness in which nobody resolves upon anything" (BT, 299). In being-unto-death Dasein is for the first time authentically *with* other Dasein inasmuch as it finally begins to live in its own skin (BT, 344). Authenticity changes the whole of Dasein's comportment to the world. This is not merely an "internal" change of view, nor is it reducible to a changed orientation to other Dasein. To paraphrase Wittgenstein: nothing in the world changes; the world as a whole changes. Heidegger unveils the secret to factical freedom in a cryptic term, *der Augenblick*, which is the German word for "instant" or "nick of time." Macquarie translates it as "the moment of vision." The etymology reveals Heidegger's sense of the term: *Augen*, meaning "eye," and *blick*, meaning "glance." The moment of vision is the glance of the eye into the "authentic present," the flash of time caught in its transition between past and future, a sudden and unmistakable grasp of facticity. "That *Present* which is held in authentic temporality and which thus is *authentic* itself, we call 'the *moment of vision*.' . . . the moment of vision permits us to encounter for the first time what can be 'in a time' as ready-to-hand or present-at-hand" (BT, 338).

Stylistically something changes in division 2 of *Being and Time.* The language, which had been monotonously analytical in division 1, becomes charged with existential angst, passion, and inspiration. Heidegger's phenomenology of death draws from springs that run much deeper in the Western tradition than Husserl or Kant. The religious preoccupations of Heidegger's youth — his deep meditation on Christian mystical and ascetical literature — resurface here transformed and secularized, but recognizable nonetheless. Eckhart, Kierkegaard, and Luther are not far in the background. The Eckhartian mystic is *gelassen;* he lets be and ceases to presume that he is the author of his righteousness or the architect of his salvation, surrendering to the hidden ground of his being. The Kierkegaardian "knight of faith," having overcome the infinite resignation of the religious stage, no longer pines for release from this transient and tear-drenched life and is so entirely "in this world" but not "of it" that he passes for a philistine. The Lutheran Christian masters himself by remembering death. In a sermon of Luther's (one Heidegger doubtlessly read) it is written: "The summons of death comes to us all, and no one dies for another. Every one must fight his own battle with death by himself, alone. We can shout into another's ears, but every one must himself be prepared for the time of death, for I will not be with you then, nor you with me."[10] Through his remembrance of death the Christian comes to his senses: the folly of sensuality, the addictive pursuit of pleasure, the vanities of the world — wealth, honor, fame — wilt in the face of death. Heidegger's Zen-like turn to "the moment of vision," seeing facticity as though for the first time, is a secular residue of this religious experience: by owning its futural gaze (we are always on some level preoccupied with death anyway), Dasein achieves an integrity that nothing else can give to it; it becomes itself.

Only one-third of *Being and Time* (as outlined in Heidegger's introduction) was written. Heidegger planned a study in six divisions divided equally into two parts; the book that was published constitutes divisions 1 and 2 of part 1. The subsequent four divisions were to lead beyond the anthropological entry point in the Dasein analytic, through a destructive

10. Martin Luther, "Eight Sermons at Wittenberg, 1522," trans. John W. Doberstein, in *Luther's Works,* vol. 51 (Philadelphia: Fortress, 1980), 70.

reading of the history of ontology, and into an interrogation of the being of time itself. Why could Heidegger not finish the project? Some argue that *Being and Time* was abandoned because Heidegger recognized soon after publishing divisions 1 and 2 that the phenomenological approach was hopelessly unsuited to ontology. These readers reference "the turn" *(Kehre)* in Heidegger's thinking in the 1930s, when he abandons the phenomenological-existential method in favor of a mythopoetic meditation upon the appearances of being. It may be, too, that the task Heidegger sets for himself in *Being and Time* is in fact impossible. Heidegger's abandonment of the project one-third of the way through may itself be a formal indication of the impossibility of providing adequate philosophical terms for life as we live it. In his readings of the history of philosophy Heidegger never pretends to have the final word on any matter. He is incessantly speaking about "preliminary" investigations, "preparing the ground," or finding access to "the question." He describes his own collected writings as "ways," not "works." To think, for Heidegger, is not to drive down a highway toward a clear destination with a good road map or global positioning; rather, it is to follow a path in the forest, which may lead to other paths — or peter out altogether.

CHAPTER 3

Ontology

Despite Heidegger's intention to provide a phenomenology faithful to life, *Being and Time* is a cumbersome, jargon-laden read: he generates theory when he aims at something akin to poetry. He wishes to give the *logoi* of phenomena, to articulate the language native to things. In the end, however, his phenomenological method, with its fastidious attention to distinction and structure, sabotages his subject matter. Heidegger abandons the technical language of *Being and Time* immediately after the book's publication; his thinking thereafter becomes increasingly experimental, and in his later writings, openly poetic. He comes to recognize that the task of thinking is impeded not merely by the theoretical attitude of some philosophers, but by philosophy itself. This shift in approach (less a change in direction than a renewed emphasis on the question of being) enables Heidegger to divest this question of the methodological and metaphysical assumptions intrinsic to existential phenomenology. The path of philosophy in Heidegger's later writings converges with poetry; what is said is subordinated to how it is said. The later Heidegger uses repetition, equivocation, and metaphor, deliberately blurring distinctions between key concepts in order to break the hold of calculative reasoning. The impressionistic language annihilates our expectations of what philosophical discourse should be.

Although it takes shape in the context of his polemic with Husserl, the question of the meaning of being develops out of Heidegger's research in medieval philosophy. Heidegger was awakened to ontology as a seminarian when he poured himself into a book by Franz Brentano, *On the Several Senses of Being in Aristotle,* given to him by a priest who sensed the boy's need for stronger than typical seminarian fare. Aristotle teaches that being can be spoken of in many ways; it is an analogy rather than a univocal concept. When I say "Socrates is my friend," I do something different with the copula than when I say "It is going to rain." An analogy according to Aristotle is a word with varying, hierarchically related senses. One of these senses is the primary meaning of the word, from which other meanings are derived and which is in turn presupposed by derivative meanings. The primary sense of being for Aristotle is substance, as in the sentence "Socrates is a man." Here we classify a substance, Socrates, according to its class (man, the species of rational animal). The other senses of being express the variety of ways that things can be related to substance. For example, I might say that "Socrates is bald." "Baldness" is not a substance but the quality of a substance, and as such it presupposes substance: "baldness" could not exist without a head. Aristotle argues that only substances truly *are* in the full sense of "being"; other things are said of substances. As proof he points to the fact that everything must be predicated of substance, but substance cannot be predicated of anything. Substances are irreducibly singular, never shared by other things.

Is ontology reducible to substance and its properties? Are the many ways of speaking of things exhausted by Aristotle's categories? Heidegger was attracted to Duns Scotus because of the latter's answer in the negative to this question. It is not enough to speak of substance; according to Scotus, we need also to speak of the singularity of the thing, its thisness or *haecceitas,* which is neither substance nor an attribute of substance. In his 1915 *Habilitationsschrift* Heidegger writes: "A doctrine of categories confined to the ten Aristotelian categories is not only incomplete, but unstable and inaccurate in its determination, because it lacks consciousness of the differences of its domains, and thus consciousness of the difference that arises from the nature of domains that are determined by the meaning-differentiations of categorial forms. It was known to Scotus too that the ten traditional categories are valid only for actual reality. Doubtless, the domain of the intentional calls for other structures" (GA1, 287-88). *The Doctrine of Categories and Meaning in Duns Scotus* is not without reason the least read of Heidegger's works. With little sign of the originality and daring that characterize Heidegger's lectures and writings of the 1920s, the book is a plodding elaboration of phenomenological prototypes in Scotistic metaphysics and medieval philosophy of language. Medievalists are inclined to make much of the fact that one of Heidegger's source texts, the *Grammatica Speculativa,* long believed to be a work of Duns Scotus, was in fact written by Thomas of Erfurt. Heidegger never commented on this error, which was discovered in 1922; we can assume that he believed it to be insignificant. The aim of Heidegger's Scotus book is not to argue for the unity of the latter's corpus, nor even to offer an exegesis of his thought, but rather to show the relevance of medieval metaphysics to phenomenology. The book is the missing link between Heidegger's training in medieval philosophy and his apprenticeship to Husserl. Heidegger not too successfully endeavors to give a phenomenological reading of Scotus, emphasizing the latter's sensitivity to the richness of the concrete and the limitations of abstract thinking.

While an ambivalent reference to the scholastic doctrine of transcendentals appears in *Being and Time* (the notion of being as a *transcendens* is one of the ontological prejudices that has led to the contemporary forgetting of the question of being [BT, 3]), Heidegger's earliest investigation of Scotus's doctrine of being does not problematize the latter's view that being is the most universal of all concepts. In 1915 Heidegger's star, it seems, had not yet risen on his intellectual horizon. Heidegger looks in some detail at how being for Scotus is a supracategorical term, which, along with unity and truth, must be said of everything that can be the subject of further predication. It is not a category because it does not distinguish the thing of which it is predicated from anything else. When I say that blue is a color, I distinguish it from mailboxes, kittens, sounds, and textures. When I say that blue *is,* I do not distinguish it at all: I say only that it is capable of further predication. In *Being and Time* Heidegger observes that the mystery barely concealed by this logical point — namely, that being is attributable to everything without having any clear significance in itself — is totally overlooked in modern philosophy. We should include also Heidegger's own *Habilitiationsschrift* among such missed opportunities to problematize the meaning of being. In *Being and Time* Heidegger corrects his oversight by pointing out that the medievals have the advantage over the moderns of not neglecting the question of being, even if they themselves made few advances on Aristotle. "So if it is said that 'Being' is the most universal concept [Scotus's position], this cannot mean that it is the one which is clearest or that it needs no further discussion. It is rather the darkest of all" (BT, 3).

On the first page of *Being and Time* appears the leitmotif of all of Heidegger's mature work in the form of a citation from Plato's *Sophist:* "For manifestly you have long been aware of what you mean when you use the expression 'being.' We, however, who used to think we understood it, have now become perplexed." Heidegger follows this passage with a commentary: "Do we in our time have an answer to the question of what we really mean by the word 'being'? Not at all. So, it is fitting that we should raise anew the question of the meaning of being. But are we nowadays even perplexed at our inability to understand the expression 'being'? Not at all. So first of all we must reawaken an understanding for the meaning of this question. Our aim in the following treatise is to work out the question of the meaning of being and to do so concretely. Our provisional aim is the interpretation of time as the possible horizon for any understanding whatsoever of being" (BT, 1). In the final sentence of this passage we find the thesis of *Being and Time:* the question of the meaning of being draws us inevitably into the question of the meaning of time. Time is more than the measure of moments, watching the "now" tick away on the clock. Time makes possible the language of existence/nonexistence. When we speak of existence we speak of things that are, things that will be, things that have been — all with an implicit reference to ourselves as the point of reference in the temporal flux. Ontological predication appears to involve the location of things as they appear to Dasein on a time continuum constituted by Dasein's alternate projection and retention of itself. It seems that the real mystery to the question of being is the problem of time and, closely related to it, the problem of the being of Dasein, which can somehow retain and project itself.

In *Being and Time* the question of the meaning of being is elaborated phenomenologically rather than metaphysically; on first glance the question has no cosmological significance but is reduced to the confines of phenomenality or givenness to an experiencing subject. Like the interlocutors in Plato's *Sophist,* we do not know what "being" means; we are in a far worse predicament to the extent that we do not even find it perplexing that we do not know. Since we are unprepared to ask the question, we must first rediscover why the meaning of being is questionable. Heidegger's way back to the question is through an analysis of the being of the human being's Dasein in the context of everyday "fallen" ways of being-in-the-world; Dasein's degraded language and subsequent derivative understanding of things is so beclouded that it fails to see the questionability of being. The goal of *Being and Time* is not to answer the question but to raise it anew, to render something that appears to be trivial questionable again.

The question is sometimes put to me by philosophers who have no patience for Heidegger, "What does Heidegger *really* mean by 'being'?" Some commentators have endeavored to correct Heidegger's ambiguity by supplementing him with a formula doubtlessly forged out of the necessity of teaching Heidegger to undergraduates. Being for Heidegger is the "horizon of meaningfulness" that is never an object but without which there can be no objects — or it is "the temporal sense of things in relation to us." However helpful these formulae may be at a certain early stage of Heidegger interpretation — and they are not entirely false — they attain clarity at too high a price. To say that being is the horizon of meaningfulness makes Heidegger sound like a realist (which he is not); to say that it is the temporalizing mode of existence that things receive when they come into relation with Dasein makes Heidegger out to be an idealist (which he is also not). The truth is that there is no simple formula for what Heidegger means by being. Heidegger never actually defines his most important distinction in *Being and Time,* namely, the difference between the ontological and the ontic. The closest he comes to a definition appears in a footnote: "While the terms 'ontisch' ('ontical') and 'ontologisch' ('ontological') are not explicitly defined, their meanings will emerge rather clearly. Ontological inquiry is concerned primarily with Being; ontical inquiry is concerned primarily with entities and the facts about them" (BT, 11 n. 3).[1] In other words, the

1. I avoid the common tendency in English to capitalize being as a way of distinguishing being from beings. This practice is not faithful to Heidegger, for all German nouns are capitalized. More problematically, it creates the impression that we are speaking of something divine, higher, or causally related to beings, an interpretation that Heidegger is dead-set against.

"ontological" concerns being, the "ontic" concerns beings. This is not a definition as much as a grammatical rule for the use of the terms. When we are properly asking the question of the meaning of being, we are speaking ontologically. On the other hand, when we speak of things in their thinghood — things with their properties and the states of affairs in which they are found, or Dasein, not in terms of its way of being but insofar as its concrete historical situation is at issue — we are using the language of the ontic. Physics and chemistry are ontic sciences; being a Christian or an atheist is an ontic affair (it involves a relationship to the things, people, and events encountered in life). The ontological concerns beings in their being, "the being of beings." In an ontological investigation we examine neither things, nor the properties of things, nor the possibilities of life; we are doing something curiously difficult, something that has eluded most thinkers throughout the history of philosophy. According to Heidegger, even Thomas Aquinas, who apparently has a great deal to say about the being of beings, stays stuck at the ontic level. The history of philosophy, Heidegger tells us, is the history of the forgetfulness of being. Not only do we have a problem posing the question of being today, *Being and Time* reminds us that we have always elided the question.

It is curious to note that Heidegger, having insisted on the careful observation of the distinction between being and beings, so freely traverses the line separating the ontological and the ontic. In choosing Dasein as the entry point for the question of the meaning of being, Heidegger enters into the ontic to find among beings one that could provide a clue to the meaning of being. In division 2 of *Being and Time* he makes a second foray into the ontic: to complete the analytic of Dasein we must presuppose an ontic ideal of the wholeness of being-in-the-world, an "existentiell" model of what constitutes Dasein's authenticity. Heidegger cannot elaborate his ontology without recourse to the ontic. Why is Dasein to be given priority among all beings as the ontic departure point for ontology? Is it not as plausible to argue for beginning with the nonhuman, with being in its most common and obvious instantiation, namely, physical presence? Why also is an existentiell ideal to guide the analysis of being human? What is to govern the selection of this ideal from among others? What indeed *is* the ontological difference if it must be suspended both at the beginning and at the end of the ontological inquiry?

We are tempted to say that ontological difference refers simply to the difference between "being" used as a noun ("Socrates is a being") and "being" used as a verb ("Socrates is being unclear"). "Being" is the present participle of the verb "to be." Is Heidegger merely saying that we need to rethink "being" in its original sense, as a verb rather than a substantive or a verbal noun? But if that is the whole of it, what then is the relationship between the ontological difference understood as a grammatical distinction and that between the being of Dasein and the being of other beings? Such deliberately cultivated ambiguities in *Being and Time* are for obvious reasons infuriating to analytically trained philosophers. Throwing up his hands in fury, one of them writes: "What are we to think of a philosopher who raises pompously and ponderously an illegibly central question in philosophy and ends up telling us that we cannot answer it, indeed cannot understand the question. How can Heidegger claim to be able to raise a question that nobody understands?"[2] It may be that Heidegger's question is not intended for answer; it may be that the question is designed to break down our comprehension, creating confusion, an incapacity to proceed with business as usual. If we are all involved in a way of thinking that elides the truth, the task for the philosopher is to disabuse us of our delusions, to take away our knowledge. On this reading, the ambiguity generated by Heidegger is not, then, the chaos generated by unclear thinking, but a deliberate and skillfully executed obfuscation — like a Zen koan — designed to break our heads and free us of the hardened categories that obstruct genuine understanding.

Werner Marx argues that Heidegger's ontology is best understood as an opposition to both premodern and modern ontological paradigms.[3] The former, derived from Aristotle, posits being as substance; the latter, beginning with Descartes, posits being as subject. Marx's astute observation touches the nerve of Heidegger's thinking. From his earliest re-

2. Herman Philipse, *Heidegger's Philosophy of Being: A Critical Interpretation* (Princeton: Princeton University Press, 1998), 8.

3. Werner Marx, *Heidegger and the Tradition,* trans. Theodore Kiseil and Murray Greene (Evanston, Ill.: Northwestern University Press, 1971), 3-14.

searches Heidegger wished to extricate philosophy from the sterile idealism-realism debate.[4] For a realist the nonsubjective has primacy over subjectivity; for an idealist it is just the reverse. Heidegger removes the conditions of the possibility of both by annulling the concepts of substance and subject. The hidden common ground underlying these two derivative concepts is for Heidegger considerably more significant than their surface tensions. Substance and subject end up censoring time insofar as they represent being in terms of constant presence. Substance underlies and lends support to change; subjectivity accompanies every mental event and thus unifies the conscious field. Aristotle sets the agenda for late antiquity and the Middle Ages by identifying being as that which possesses attributes or qualities. Descartes sets the agenda for modernity by designating being as subjectivity. The so-called opposing schools of modern empiricism and modern rationalism both agree that the subject underlies all mental events and makes possible the unity of experience.

Already in the *Habilitationsschrift,* Heidegger said the main problem with Aristotle's metaphysics of substance was that it painted everything with one brush. In Aristotle's hands the human being, with its strikingly nonsubstantial modes of being, gets strictly interpreted in terms of a finite set of substances and accidents. Heidegger's corrective here is Dasein, an entity to which the concept of substance fails to apply insofar as Dasein's distinctive qualities cannot be found in any substance: unlike

---

4. See Heidegger's letter to Rickert, 24 April 1914, in *Martin Heidegger/Heinrich Rickert. Briefe 1912 bis 1933,* ed. Alfred Denker (Frankfurt am Main: Vittorio Klostermann, 2002), 17-18: "Your valuable input with respect to Duns Scotus, to understand and evaluate him through the medium of modern logic, has encouraged me to make a first, and in any case, preliminary attempt to retrieve his 'language logic.' In the meantime, I have learned to see that a real doctrine of meaning lies at its basis, which can be illuminated by the doctrine of meaning and categories in 'transcendental empiricism.' I soon saw that restricting myself to this great tractate will not lead me to full understanding, and therefore, I started to study the great commentaries on Aristotle's logic and metaphysics. I was able to distinguish the levels of the domains of being, meaning, and knowledge, which I believe were not maintained before transcendental philosophy, the point where, as far as I can see, 'realism' must be essentially transformed. First of all, the needy fear of 'subjectivism' — which has become the etiquette of every non-extreme Thomistic 'standpoint' — must be eliminated."

other beings, Dasein circles around its being, anticipating its future on the basis of its retention of its past, and retaining its past on the basis of its anticipation of the future. The modern category of subjectivity fares no better. Subjectivity is being that exists for itself in relation to itself. Its advantage over substance is that it can have a past and a future. The one thing that is indubitable in our experience, Descartes tells us, and is hence the only candidate for the foundation of all certain knowledge, is subjectivity: I can doubt that the world exists and I can doubt that I have a body, but I cannot doubt that I think. Cartesian subjectivity is the "I" that thinks whatever it happens to think, the ego that undergirds everything that can be thought or said. In Kant subjectivity becomes the condition of the possibility of experience; in German idealism it becomes the condition of the possibility of the world itself. For Husserl, subjectivity is the horizon of the given; everything that is given is given for subjectivity. According to Heidegger, everything becomes an object for subjective acts of knowing and willing when the self is interpreted as subject; ontology becomes locked into egology. Nonnoetic experiences such as moods or the everyday understanding of our work world are marginalized for having limited ontological significance. And yet, Heidegger says, it is precisely in terms of nonnoetic experiences that the primacy of temporality is inevitable. Subjectivity is another effort to censor time by defining being in terms of something, or better, someone, who does not change.

The idolatry of substance/subject is no innocent mistake in the history of philosophy, but a strategy to avoid thinking about the temporality of being-in-the-world, a compulsion rooted in Dasein's "fallenness." Although Heidegger is no fan of Freud, it is no accident that *Being and Time* comes on the scene at the beginning of the psychoanalytic century. One notices that division 1 is subtitled "The Dasein Analytic." Heidegger believes, following Freud, that the human being is in the grip of what Ricoeur calls "false consciousness."[5] Dasein must be interpreted against itself; its self-understanding cannot be trusted. In what amounts to a secularization of Luther's *aversio Dei,* Heidegger speaks of Dasein as being-in-the-untrue: "Because Dasein is essentially falling, its state of Being is

5. Paul Ricoeur, *Freud and Philosophy: An Essay on Interpretation,* trans. Denis Savage (New Haven: Yale University Press, 1970), 33.

such that it is in 'untruth'" (BT, 222). Truth must be wrested from situations in which the uncovered is always threatened with being covered over again. Dasein has a tendency to conceal the truth, to invent fictions, and to employ strategies for avoiding truth: "idle talk" (chatter that presumes to have understood while barring access to understanding); "curiosity" (the search for diversion and novelty); and metaphysics itself (a discourse that locates the meaning of being outside of time). Heidegger searches for a hermeneutic foothold, a vantage point from which to deconstruct the history of philosophy in order to expose the very thing that is most burdensome for Dasein to hold before itself, namely, time and death. Freud tells us that we repress things that threaten the ego. The meaning of being in Heidegger is similarly "repressed" insofar as it threatens the illusion we perpetuate about ourselves, namely, that time and death will not consume our being in the end. Like the repressed trauma in Freudian analysis that precedes the formation of the ego and remains ever outside the analysand's experience, the temporal sense of being is buried under layers of nontemporal conceptions constitutive of both culture and self-understanding. To free them up requires nothing short of a wholesale disassembly *(Destruktion)* of the Western mind.

Dasein's nonsubstantiality — whether substance be conceived classically as the capacity to support attributes or as a subject unifying experience by sustaining the flow of consciousness — is revealed through an analysis of Dasein's relationship to time. The phenomenon of this relationship is never adequately thematized, in Heidegger's view, even if there have been occasional historical indications: Aristotle's definition of time refers to one who measures the passage of moments;[6] Augustine interprets time as an "extension of the soul" *(distentio animi);*[7] and Kant

6. Aristotle, *Physics*, trans. R. P. Hardie and R. K. Gaye, in *The Basic Works of Aristotle*, ed. Richard McKeon (New York: Random House, 1941), 4.10.219b1: "For time is just this-number of motion in respect of before and after." Heidegger lectured on this definition of time, drawing attention to how "the before and after" imply a horizon of primordial, experienced time, which in turn refers to Dasein's fore-theoretical experience, in GA24, 232-56.

7. Augustine, *Confessions*, trans. Henry Chadwick (New York: Oxford University Press, 1991), 11.20: "Perhaps it would be exact to say: there are three times, a present of things past, a present of things present, a present of things to come. In the soul there are these three aspects of time, and I do not see them anywhere else. The present considering the

deduces time as the formal condition of all subjective intuitions.[8] Phenomenological reflection shows how Dasein is the product of its past; it is what it has become. On deeper reflection, however, Heidegger reveals that the past is a function of the future: Dasein is being-toward-future, an anticipation of its being, and a projection of itself upon its possibilities. Only in the light of anticipation does the past come into view as determinative of existence. Dasein finds itself "thrown" *(geworfen)* — in the midst of other Dasein and "innerworldly things" that it does not create or control — into moods, horizons of interpretation, and historical discourses that began prior to its arrival and will continue after it is gone. Dasein comes up against this thrownness in its projection of itself *(der Entwurf)* into the possible. These primordial experiences of the past and future do not merely condition Dasein's being (as though Dasein were a substance that is in time, but need not be); Dasein is nothing other than a "thrown projection" *(geworfener Entwurf)*.

All of Dasein's "existentials" or recurring ontological features have a temporal significance. Existence can be distinguished from the "presence in the present" of so-called real things on the grounds of its reference to possibility, that is, futurity. Dasein exists, which means it is a "to-be" *(zu-sein)* in a temporal sense: Dasein is a being toward possibility, a being always *to be* actualized. Dasein's being is always outstanding as a yet-to-be-achieved actualization; its essence stands before it as a project (in both senses, as something to be done, and as something cast out ahead of oneself). Dasein's projection of itself onto possibility drives it back into its origins in a restless circling around its being. "Attunement" indicates the primordial pastness of Dasein, the thrownness of being-in-the-world: Dasein always already finds itself in a particular emotional

---

past is the memory, the present considering the present is immediate awareness, the present considering the future is expectation." Heidegger lectured on this text to a cloister of monks at Beuron, near Messkirch, in 1930. The lecture is still unpublished.

8. Immanuel Kant, *Critique of Pure Reason,* trans. Norman Kemp Smith (New York: Palgrave Macmillan, 2003), A 34, B 50: "Just as I can say *a priori* that all outer appearances are in space, and are determined *a priori* in conformity with the relations of space, I can also say, from the principle of inner sense, that all appearances whatsoever, that is, all objects of the senses, are in time, and necessarily stand in time-relations." Heidegger examined this text in his 1929 book *Kant and the Problem of Metaphysics,* trans. Richard Taft (Bloomington: Indiana University Press, 1997), 34-36.

attunement, discovers itself responding to a world that it does not constitute, and in ways that elude its own theoretical grasp. "Understanding" indicates Dasein's primordial futurity or projective power. Dasein "knows" its way around its world on the basis of anticipatory projections of possible ways for it to be in the world. Time is no longer considered a physical condition in which Dasein exists, alongside other things equally subject to change; rather, Dasein "temporalizes" being in its retention of itself, its presencing, and its projection of itself onto possibility. This temporalizing power of Dasein must not be interpreted as something that I do; it is something that happens to me. I am as much thrown into a future as I am thrown into a past. The possible does not emerge from pure nothingness but from concrete dispensations of possibility given in my past. "Since the Dasein always comes toward-itself from out of a possibility of itself, it therewith also always comes-back-to what it has been. Having-been-ness, the past in the existential sense, belongs with equal originality to the future in the original (existential) sense" (GA24, 265).

Dasein's primordial past, present, and future merge into a unified experience of historicity, an experience Heidegger calls "ecstatic horizonal temporality," an apocalyptic structure that differs from clock time as anticipation differs from expectation. Clock time is theoretical and deworlded time, the measurement of objectified "now" points that shuttle along a time line from a nonexistent past through an extensionless present and into a nonexistent future. The now is abstracted from what went before and what is yet to come. Ecstatic horizonal temporality is not constituted by a static "now"; it is a unified field of being stretching alongside my having been, my now being, and my ability to be. Past, present, and future are three mutually interpenetrating modes of the self-transcendence of Dasein, three "ecstasies" that interpenetrate and imply each other. Heidegger is driven into increasingly obscure formulations to articulate this single horizon of past, present, and future. It is "the enpresenting-foregone-Future" *(die gewesend-gegenwärtige Zukunft),* the reversal of our commonsense understanding of the linear movement of time (from out of a past, through a present, toward a future): Dasein moves from out of a future through a past toward a present: "Expecting a possibility, I come from this possibility toward that which I myself am. The Dasein, expecting its ability to be, comes toward itself" (GA24, 265).

The later Heidegger abandons phenomenological method and with it the anthropocentric frame, but he deepens, through a series of revisions of Greek terms, the identification of ontology and temporality that is the theme of *Being and Time*. This is not a return to metaphysics; Heidegger has ruled out thinking the being of beings without Dasein. It is rather an effort to think being in a way that has never before been thought: not from the perspective of Dasein, or from the perspective of God, or from a third-person objective viewpoint, but from within the ontological difference itself. The difficulty this task presents to thinking comes to the fore in Heidegger's transitional essay, the 1929 "What Is Metaphysics?" Logic fails utterly before the horrific and unthinkable convergence of nothingness and being. The horizon of beings, the condition of the possibility of the totality of things that are and could be, is not substance or act but nothingness. Some Heideggerian Thomists, inspired by the rigor of Heidegger's insistence on the ontological difference (which they confuse with Aquinas's distinction between *esse* and *essentia*), point out that *esse* can also be interpreted as "the nothing" because it is not a thing but a no-thing, a surpassing of all things. For Aquinas, however, *actus purus* is fullness, not emptiness, an infinite *plenum* that grounds and makes possible the reality of particular beings. Heidegger's *Nichts* (nothingness) is not the fullness that precedes all coming-to-be, erotically drawing all things back to itself; it is the lack that renders coming-to-be unthinkably contingent, ungrounded and repellent to reason. Aquinas's human being is a reaching for absolute being, irresistibly attracted to it as the good that everything desires to possess: "the human being is directed to God as to an end which exceeds the grasp of his reason."[9] Dasein is anxious, forlorn, repelled, perhaps even absurd, a "being held out into the nothing" (WM, 108). The question at the origin of Western philosophy, "Why is there something rather than nothing?" would never have occurred to us, says Heidegger, if the nothing were not hovering over everything as the source and fate of things that come to be. The nothing is the negation of the totality of beings; it precedes every negation; it is even more original than the

9. Thomas Aquinas, *Summa Theologica* (New York: Benzinger Bothers, 1947), 1a, q. 1, a. 1.

"not." It is not only that the nothing makes possible the negating of everything; it makes possible the *thinking* of everything — it *is* the transcendental condition. Notice just how revolutionary Heidegger's position is. We have already spoken of the break with the scholastics. In his thinking about the nothing, Heidegger is also breaking with modernity. For Descartes, Kant, and Husserl, that which makes possible finite being, both mental and material, is (respectively) God, the unconditioned, and transcendental subjectivity. Heidegger is saying that the transcendental condition of the possibility of Dasein and the beings that show themselves to it is nothingness; more accurately, there is no transcendental ground. In a 1956 lecture on the dictum of the seventeenth-century German mystic Angelius Silesius, "the rose is without why,"[10] Heidegger endeavors to think that which is seemingly unthinkable: being without cause or explanation.

Heidegger's critique of technology, a high point in his later work, represents a return to sociopolitical concerns after his loss of face as a defrocked Nazi professor. The aging philosopher, who grew up in a farm town and spent his happiest days in a hut in the Black Forest, was genuinely saddened by the breakneck speed of change and technological transformation sweeping across Germany in the aftermath of the Second World War. The people were forced to rebuild their medieval towns and cities from rubble, and aesthetic and architectural considerations gave way to economic imperatives: concrete and steel buildings were erected over medieval town squares; freeways were plowed through bucolic valleys; rivers were dammed for hydroelectrical power. The mobilization of people, the mass media, and a general fascination with all things American lured the German mind away from its declining culture, of which many younger Germans were ashamed because of its ubiquitous association with the Holocaust. Heidegger speaks out in the midst of this rapid cultural transformation. Technology is not neutral, he warns, nor is it a tool at our disposal that we can use without regard for its consequences: "Everywhere we remain unfree and chained to technology, whether we passionately affirm or deny it. But we are delivered over to it in the worst

---

10. Martin Heidegger, *The Principle of Reason*, trans. Reginald Lilly (Bloomington: Indiana University Press, 1991), 42.

possible way when we regard it as something neutral; for this conception of it, to which today we particularly like to do homage, makes us utterly blind to the essence of technology" (QT, 287).

"The Question concerning Technology" begins with a variation on Aristotle's distinction between things that come to be through *physis* and things that come to be through human artifice or *technē*. From an acorn grows the oak. But if I plant a table in the garden, it will not grow into another table. The oak holds within itself the secret of its emergence while the table, which depends on human *technē* to come into being, does not. *Physis* is a spontaneous coming into the light of being from a place of darkness. Heidegger believes that we have never before thought *physis* in its dynamism. We think of a thing as an essence, a being with a nature that defines it, and so fail to think of it as the trace of a passage of being from nothing. Playing on Aristotle's notion of *technē* as a mode of knowing, technology, Heidegger says, is a certain revelation of beings, a concentration on the thing as a separate being, an essence, something with properties that can be broken down into its parts. Technology reveals beings as reducible to structure, analyzable, quantifiable, and controllable. Heidegger corrects the shortsightedness of modern natural science, which tends to conceive of seventeenth-century science as an absolute beginning: we could not have arrived at planetary technology without the history of metaphysics. Socrates' search for "forms," essential definitions, is the beginning of a path that leads inexorably to nuclear fission. In the age of global technology, *technē* severs its roots in *physis* and labors, however absurdly, to set the agenda for the emergence and withdrawal of things from the nothing; beings are no longer permitted to follow their own internal rhythm but are coerced into constant presence. A culture whose *technē* is in dialogue with *physis* (Heidegger romanticizes pretechnological farm life) does not control or dominate the presence of beings, but waits for the event of their emergence. *Physis* requires that one adjust to the emergence of things in their own time and of their own accord, and make provisions for their inevitable withdrawal. Modern *technē*, by contrast, makes everything available all the time (fresh greens in winter, fresh salmon every day of the week): nothing comes to be or disappears on its own because we have reduced everything to something that is constantly available, what Heidegger calls a "stock" or a "standing reserve" (QT, 322).

When we realize that truth *(alētheia)* follows the rhythm of emergence and withdrawal, we see the ways in which technological thinking imperils Dasein — so susceptible, in its fallenness, to self-deception and falsehood — by promoting a truncated understanding of beings. Since calculative thinking cannot tolerate a truth that emerges and withdraws on its own, it substitutes its own criterion for truth: quantity or mathematicable presence. The situation as Heidegger sees it is dire: the problems precipitated by technology cannot be solved by more calculation. Heidegger was particularly worried about nuclear power, but he would certainly draw on even more disturbing examples if he were writing today. The way forward as Heidegger sees it will come to us (if it comes at all) like grace, wholly from without, the in-breaking of that which we could never achieve within the system, that which represents the system's other, a "saving power." Our task is to ready ourselves to receive this saving power by practicing technological asceticism, reserving for ourselves the freedom to say no to technology. *Gelassenheit,* which plays a minor role in *Being and Time,* emerges in the later writings as the principal Heideggerian "virtue." The word is untranslatable, but a rough paraphrase would be "the quality of letting be," or literally, "letting-be-ness."

The later Heidegger's ontology revolves around another untranslatable German word: *Ereignis.*[11] Approximated as "the event," "enowning," or "appropriating," *Ereignis* is an overdetermined word. It connotes the happening — the rupture or opening — that holds within itself the secret of its happening and makes possible both Dasein and the appearance of beings dependent upon its "disclosedness" or openness *(Erschlossenheit).* It also connotes the appropriation of facticity or owning of one's time, a task that belongs uniquely to Dasein. The difficulty with the term *Ereignis* is that it references two seemingly incompatible ideas: the notion of an event and the notion of appropriation. The former appears to be an objective happening, the latter a subjective act, something one does. The ambiguity is of course deliberate. Dasein's owning of itself,

11. Between 1936 and 1938 Heidegger worked on a manuscript that he considered to be his magnum opus and yet hesitated to publish for fear of being misunderstood. It was published posthumously in 1989 under the title *Beiträge zu Philosophy (Vom Ereignis)* [GA65: *Contributions to Philosophy (From Enowning)*]. The work is among Heidegger's most obscure.

which is the task for thinking and the only experience of truth available to us, is the event of history. The later Heidegger clarifies that the thinking that begins with *Being and Time* is neither directed to being in a metaphysical sense (the whatness or thatness of things) nor directed to the human being in an existential-phenomenological sense. Its theme is the coincidence of Dasein with the appearance of beings, whose self-showing is only for Dasein. "The human being is the shepherd of being called by being itself into the preservation of being's truth" (GA9, 260). This leads Heidegger to ask, what makes possible both the showing of beings and the being for whom beings are shown? The question strikes us as extraordinarily abstract because it is no longer working within any of the received philosophical narratives: being is no longer out there (realism), nor in here (idealism); the human being is no longer one among many things subject to physical or metaphysical conditions, nor is the human being the ground of the world. The later Heidegger expends all his energies on breaking the presuppositions operating in these narratives. *Physis* is not the prehuman appearance of things, even for the early Greeks. Rather *physis* is the spontaneous emergence of things for Dasein: being and appearance of being to Dasein coincide.

The mystery of this convergence raises two further questions: What kind of being is Dasein that it can be the site for the appearance of beings? (This is the question of *Being and Time.*) Secondly, what is the condition of the possibility of the interdependence of beings and human being? What opens up Dasein as the site of the appearance of beings? The answer to the last question is *Ereignis:* the "event" simultaneously opens the clearing (the not) that is Dasein and makes possible the appearance of beings. We can now see more clearly where Heidegger is heading with his notion of ontological guilt in *Being and Time:* only insofar as the human being is defined by a lack of being, insofar as it is not coincident with its being (in that its being is always an issue for it), is the temporal space secured for the appearance of beings. Without presuming to have found the formula of the later Heidegger (there is no formula), we can make a few thematic observations. Inasmuch as *alētheia* is the unveiling of beings that is preceded and succeeded by a return into darkness and *physis* remains horizoned by the nothing that shows itself as the spontaneous and contingent emergence of things from out of themselves, *Ereignis* is Dasein's irruption into being in its sheer unmasterable eventfulness, the incalculable happening of Dasein's disclosedness. The experience of *Ereignis* pulsates with the vital threefold relationship of Dasein, being, and temporality, a relationship that Heidegger so laboriously tries to retrieve in *Being and Time.* *Ereignis* names that which is never unveiled to calculation, that which is repeatedly suppressed by the metaphysics of presence, namely, the unthinkable upsurge in the nothing that renders Dasein free and available for the showing of being.

The history of metaphysics, which coincides with the history of technology and the history of Western civilization, is the repeated effort to repress *Ereignis.* Technology has its roots in Greek philosophy with the fatal turn in Socrates, Plato, and Aristotle away from *physis* to a metaphysics privileging presence over absence, eternity over time, and substance over nothingness. The divine being is configured by Plato as the good, by Aristotle as pure act, in both instances an absolute self-presence capable of protecting the totality of beings from the danger of *Ereignis.* Greek philosophical monotheism consolidates the move from *physis* to metaphysics, merging with the revelation of the one God in the Jewish Bible into a monolithic tradition Heidegger calls "onto-theology." Used as a synonym for metaphysics, onto-theology conceals the question of the meaning of being by constructing a narrative that traces all beings back to a highest being, the good, the first mover, the Creator, the first cause or the *causa sui.* In Heidegger's view it is no accident that most metaphysical treatises in the history of Western philosophy are founded on a philosophy of God. Metaphysics, Heidegger says, is essentially onto-theological: it allows us to elide the question of the meaning of being by presenting the origin of beings as a foregone conclusion: we always already know where beings come from (God); hence we can, with seemingly good conscience, limit our thinking to the ontic.

The eventfulness of *Ereignis* is experienced in the vicissitudes of history, no moment of which gives us an absolute vantage point from which preceding epochs may be judged; every age brings with it unprecedented disclosures and concomitant concealments of what has been disclosed. We are "sent" *(geschickt)* into an epoch of history in which being opens up the "there" of a historical moment of Dasein and makes possible a set of possibilities for understanding while closing down others — the later Heidegger's version of "the hermeneutical situation." The early Heidegger tells us that we neither can nor should want to extricate ourselves from that into which we have been thrown: to understand is to think our way into the strengths and limits of the way of seeing constitutive of our time. For the later Heidegger an original "sending" of being is progressively distorted and forgotten until, at the end of the epoch, oblivion descends upon Dasein and the old traditions no longer speak to it. Heidegger's philosophy of history is a story not of continual progress but of inevitable decline. The task for "thinking" (the successor to philosophy) is to decipher the meaning of the Western epoch as it winds itself down. "The latecomers" await in darkness the new sending, which will open the new era of thinking. When the sun rises in the Black Forest, that which was not seen clearly emerges into the light: the valley, the farmhouses, and the animals come into clear illumination. At the same time, something disappears that prior to this unconcealment was unconcealed, namely, the stars in the night sky.

The later Heidegger's predilection for the language of destiny is a natural development of the antiliberalism of *Being and Time* and the political writings of the 1930s. Conscious of the political disaster of his Nazi involvement, the later Heidegger makes a point of freeing the notion of destiny from any nationalistic interpretation. Where in *Being and Time* destiny is discussed in terms of ethnic and cultural heritage, in the later work destiny is expanded to include the whole human race, a point that comes clearly to the fore in the 1946 "Letter on Humanism":

> When Hölderlin composes "Homecoming" he is concerned that his "countrymen" find their essence. He does not at all seek that essence in an egoism of his nation. He sees it rather in the context of a belongingness to the destiny of the West. But even the West is not thought regionally as the Occident in contrast to the Orient, nor merely as Europe, but rather world-historically out of nearness to the source. . . . "German" is not spoken to the world so that the world might be reformed through the German essence; rather, it is spoken to the Germans so that from a fateful belongingness to the nations they might become world-historical along with them. (LH, 241-42)

Technology is the end of Western civilization in both senses of the word "end": it represents the closure of a particular history of creative philosophical and scientific work, but also the goal of that history, that toward which the West has always been headed. At the end of "The Question concerning Technology" Heidegger cites Hölderlin's famous couplet: "Where the danger lies, there the saving power grows." At this moment of crisis when philosophy seems to have nothing more to offer and technology sets the agenda for further scientific development (when we have become "the tools of our tools"), a possibility of salvation grows at the heart of the crisis. Heidegger does not, therefore, advocate a Luddite retreat to the woods. In the technological age, hitherto inaccessible possibilities for thinking — possibilities that were once concealed in the origin — are active once again. The origin comes toward us from out of the future: the return to the origin is not simply a turn back to the past; rather, it is the return of that which was missed when we first set off on the course that has led to the present moment. Heidegger thinks of the origin as a site of multiple possibilities that become increasingly closed off as the beginning actualizes itself into a particular course of history until one eventually finds oneself with only one course of action left available. Only when the trajectory completes itself do we return to the origin, but always in a new way:

> Do we stand in the eve [*Vorabend*] of the most monstrous transformation of the whole earth and that era in which it is suspended? Do we stand on the eve of a night which heralds another dawn? . . . Is the land of the evening [*Abend-Land*] only now emerging? Will this land of evening overwhelm Occident and Orient alike, transcending whatever is merely European to become the location of a new but primordially fated history? . . . Are we the latecomers we are? But are we also at the same time precursors of the dawn of an altogether different age, which has already left our historiological representation of history behind? (GA5, 17)

John Caputo draws an important distinction between eschatological and teleological models of time, a point of some confusion for readers of Heidegger despite their being opposites, strictly speaking. In teleology the

last (the end, or *telos*) comes after the first, through a period of matura-
tion. The plant is known in its blossom. In eschatology the first overtakes
the last with an unexpected violence.[12] Teleology begins small and ends
great through a steady and progressive development; eschatology begins
great and ends small through an ineluctable decline. We in the late technological age find ourselves in the encroaching darkness following the illumination of a horizon of possibilities that occurred within Greek philosophy. We are Westerners (*Abendländer,* literally "evening dweller"), the
people of the evening; the sun that rose with the Greeks is now setting.
That which opened to the first light of dawn has spent itself. In the working out of destiny we become increasingly oblivious to what was once vital at the origins of our tradition — oblivious, that is, until we are faced —
as we are in the contemporary moment — with that tradition's decline at
a time when it has lost all standing in the culture. And yet for those with
eyes to see, the origins of Western thought are now uniquely accessible.
Calculative thinking, which Socrates defines and Plato and Aristotle per-
fect, makes modern scientific and technological development possible
even as it precipitates the atrophy of Dasein's meditative capacities. The
end of an epoch brings with it an experience of homelessness with no
sense of how to go forward. We do not feel at home in the technological
world we have made for ourselves — the eco-anxiety currently gripping
society confirms Heidegger's claim — and we have lost our trusted
guides. Heidegger believes himself called to prophetically announce the
advent of this unimaginable new epoch that is beginning to unconceal itself, at least for the poets and thinkers. A subtle sense of hope thus pervades the later Heidegger, a hope not in humanity — it is not we ourselves
who are going to renew our civilization — but in being.

12. Caputo puts it thus: "The end in question is not a teleo-linear goal and consum-
mation in which the accumulated potencies of the Western tradition reach their fulfill-
ment — quite the opposite. It is the emptying (not the filling), the spending and exhaust-
ing of a great beginning. The eschaton means we have reached the point where the
potency of the tradition has been spent, and the question is whether we will persist indefi-
nitely in this dead end or whether the eschaton will turn itself inside and out and become
the point of departure for a new beginning, an opening on to what-is-coming." John D.
Caputo, *Radical Hermeneutics: Repetition, Deconstruction, and the Hermeneutic Project*
(Bloomington: Indiana University Press, 1987), 161.

CHAPTER 4

Axiology

I use "axiology" in the title of this chapter to designate philosophical concern for the good. The suffix comes from *logos,* the Greek noun for "word," which derives from the verb *legō,* "to speak"; the prefix is derived from *axios,* the Greek adjective for "worthy." "Axiology" means literally any "speaking" of the "worthy." Understood in this original sense, axiology is not what analysts call "value-theory," a conceptual investigation into the kinds of things that can be considered bearers of value. Rather, it is the doctrine of what medieval philosophers call "wisdom": knowledge of what is right and wrong, good and bad, in both a theoretical and practical sense. In the broadest sense, axiology concerns whatever a philosopher believes to be worth pursuing in human life. By entitling this chapter "Axiology," I am calling out the early Heidegger on his alleged ethical-political neutrality. Following Husserl's presumption that phenomenology does not endorse any particular system of values over any other, Heidegger endeavors to suspend ethical and political judgment in *Being and Time,* understanding his contributions to be exclusively on the level of ontology and existential anthropology. For Heidegger, what ethics and politics do with phenomenology is their own business — provided they acknowledge their own limits and do not presume to be able to answer phenomenological questions. Heidegger's political activities in the 1930s, however, suggest that a particular ethics and politics are at least implicit in *Being and Time,* raising the question, once again, of the relation of the ontic to the ontological. If the ontological is implicitly oriented in a particular ontic direction, if certain ethical-political applications of ontology

77

are more suited than others, what becomes of the primacy of the question of being?

Heidegger's alleged Nazism has been discussed ad nauseam in the literature. No one would worry about Heidegger's rather modest political involvements if he were a minor philosopher. Since he is frequently described as "the greatest philosopher of the twentieth century," his politics cannot be ignored. Some readers reject the whole of Heidegger's philosophical project on the basis of his politics, citing the inevitable implication of *Being and Time* in authoritarian and totalitarian ways of thinking. On the other extreme, others say we must separate the politics from the man: we must distinguish Heidegger's work from his life and allow his contribution to the history of philosophy to speak for itself. Neither of these approaches is satisfying. Rejecting a work of philosophy outright because one disapproves of the philosopher's political associations can be problematic; much depends, of course, on how grounded in understanding is the nature of one's disapproval. Politics is certainly not a good reason to neglect a thinker, especially one as influential as Heidegger. On the other hand, the attempt to rigorously distinguish between the work and the life is no better. In the case of Heidegger — the philosopher of facticity for whom philosophy and existence are inseparable — the work is as appropriately read alongside the life as the life is alongside the work.

This chapter is meant as only an introduction to axiological issues in Heidegger. I will neither defend nor condemn Heidegger's ethical-political views, reserving my critical remarks for the postscript of the book. My immediate concern is to understand Heidegger's ethical-political position and to show how it is consistent with the ontology of *Being and Time.* I look first at the ontological foundation for ethics provided in *Being and Time,* and secondly at Heidegger's lived politics as they emerge in the speeches and writings of his Nazi period (1933-45). The later Heidegger, who gets short shrift in this chapter, left Nietzschean decisionism behind him and rediscovered, along with a theological voice, some kind of social conscience. This postwar Heidegger repudiates the Nietzschean will to power for being enmeshed in metaphysics (albeit its last gasp). He also comes to locate National Socialism and the Second World War within the destiny of technological civilization, a civilization he deems to be the catastrophic expression of the modern effort to rationalize life. Disturbingly, the later Heidegger does not see the Holocaust as evil so much as symptomatic of the excesses of technological civilization. In one of his few references to the Holocaust, a 1949 lecture entitled "Das Ge-Stell," Heidegger writes: "Agriculture is now a motorized food-industry — in essence, the same as the manufacturing of corpses in gas chambers and extermination camps, the same as the blockading and starving of nations [the Berlin blockade was then active], the same as the manufacture of hydrogen bombs."[1] Far from a return to humanism or liberalism, this later Heidegger launches a fresh attack on both from a new angle: theo-ecology.

The Husserlian term *épochè* means "suspension" in the sense of bracketing (which is different from annulling or negating). Heidegger performs an *épochè* on ethical and political questions in *Being and Time*. Heidegger's methodological reticence to speak of good and evil, right and wrong, and justice and injustice is in part symptomatic of his era. We find similar moratoriums on axiology not only in Husserl but also in Bertrand Russell, Ludwig Wittgenstein, and Karl Popper. According to these thinkers, philosophy does not and cannot offer guidance on how to live and govern. The best philosophy can do is clarify the terms that might emerge in any such discussion. For a variety of social and political reasons, early-twentieth-century philosophy loses its belief in the power of philosophy to deliver wisdom or offer practical guidance.

However sympathetic I am to the climate of skepticism that distinguishes our age, I am wary of philosophers who postpone axiology. While they are busy building an ethically neutral ontology or epistemology, their own unexamined values are being inscribed into the foundation. Heidegger's alleged ethical neutrality in *Being and Time* makes it possible for him to say whatever he wants about Dasein without having to worry

1. "Ackerbau ist jetzt motorisierte Ernährungsindustrie, im Wesen das Selbe wie die Fabrikation von Leichen in Gaskammern und Vernichtungslagern, das Selbe wie die Blockade und Aushungerung von Ländern, das Selbe wie die Fabrikation von Wasserstoffbomben." Cited in Wolfgang Schirmacher, *Technik und Gelassenheit* (Freiburg: Alber, 1983), 25, from p. 25 of a typescript of the lecture. The published version of the lecture, "The Question concerning Technology," omits everything after the first five words of the sentence. See QT, 320. Translation and citation found in Thomas Sheehan, "Heidegger and the Nazis," *New York Review of Books* 35, no. 10 (16 June 1988): 38-47.

about what the ethicists or political theorists might think about it (they have been not-so-cordially ushered out of the room before the discussion even begins). Axiology is inevitable, always already going on, even in the most theoretically abstract discussions. Every treatise "on human nature" in the history of philosophy is political insofar as it advances or removes foundations for a variety of political positions. Aquinas's treatise on human nature in the *Summa Theologica* is a not-so-subtle metaphysical justification for Christian monarchy. Enlightenment ideology pours off the page of Kant's second critique.

In spite of Heidegger's methodologic "light touch" on questions of the good, *Being and Time* in effect advances a post-Christian value-system. It is difficult — for me, impossible — to regard "authenticity," "indifference," and "inauthenticity" as ethically neutral designators of alternative ways of being-in-the-world. Enthusiasts of *Being and Time* get swept up in what Adorno describes as "the jargon of authenticity," the neo-Nietzschean language of overcoming the basic duplicity in human being. They speak as though they have found in Heidegger a complete philosophy of life — and indeed they have. How can one not hear axiology in the language of "fallenness," "guilt," and "conscience"? What is surprising is not that phenomenology so quickly becomes axiology in Heidegger — in some ways this is the turn from phenomenology to existentialism that Husserl, for all his protests, could not prevent. The surprise is Heidegger's artlessness about the move. His numerous ethical and political disclaimers give the impression that he genuinely believes that his philosophy is merely descriptive rather than prescriptive. In answer to such confidence, perhaps it is enough to ask how other axiologies fare in the wake of the Dasein analytic. If Heidegger's phenomenology is neutral, it should leave everything as it was. This is not the case, of course: liberal humanism is demolished by Heidegger's collectivism; individualism is defeated by his doctrine of being-with; and Christian morality is vigorously deconstructed, its central pieces plundered for use in his reconstruction of what it means to live a genuinely human life.

To be fair, Heidegger does not believe that axiology can be suspended permanently. He differs from Wittgenstein in this respect. Heidegger does believe, however, that his phenomenological ontology prepares the ground for ethical and political work. In this sense *Being and Time* contains something analogous to a transcendental ethics. Like Kant's *Groundwork for the Metaphysics of Morals,* the Dasein analytic is meant to describe without content or detail the formal structure of human life within which a variety of different axiological positions can potentially be developed. But just as ontology cannot proceed in ignorance of the ontic, so transcendental ethics cannot be indifferent to application. You cannot do ethics without first doing concrete analyses: you must at some point ground the discussion in determinate notions of good and evil, examples of ideal governments, etc. Heidegger calls this kind of work "ontic" because it is concerned not with being-in-the-world as such but with particular ways of being-in-the-world. He is not concerned with such work in *Being and Time* (at least not explicitly), but that does not mean he does not appreciate its importance. Ontology, for Heidegger, prepares the ground for ethics and politics by uncovering the ontological structures at play in any ethical-political situation. Any sound ontic discussion would ideally proceed with reference to such structures, or at the very least do well to avoid contradicting them (either by presuming to lay an alternative ontological framework or by overlooking the foundation that has already been cleared).

As we saw in chapter 2 of this book, Heidegger demonstrates that the Cartesian notion of an isolated ego is phenomenologically ungrounded. Dasein is never really alone; its being is "being-with" *(Mitsein).* Heidegger's model of intersubjectivity can be usefully contrasted with the alternative offered by the Jewish philosopher Emmanuel Levinas. According to the Levinasian critique, Heidegger fails to acknowledge the irreducible difference of the other. The others of *Being and Time* do not confront me as irreducible to my subjectivity, but are rather the they from whom I fail to distinguish myself on a regular basis. In Levinas's view, the other challenges me in the roots of my being. The face of the other is the face of one I do not understand. The other confronts me as an impenetrable abyss of difference that encroaches upon me and sets limits to my being. My inclination is to murder him; only by overcoming this desire can I enter into ethical relations with him.[2] For Heidegger, on

2. Emmanuel Levinas, *Totality and Infinity: An Essay on Exteriority,* trans. Alphonso Lingis (Pittsburgh: Duquesne University Press, 1969), 198.

the other hand, Dasein knows exactly what to expect from the others insofar as they are no different from it. The others do not confront Dasein; on the contrary, they allow Dasein to avoid the confrontation with itself that is always impending.

In the face of this critique, which has become formulaic in postmodern circles, one should qualify Heidegger's position. That Dasein is always being-with does not mean that it has no sense of itself as separate from other selves. Dasein is always defining itself in relation to the others. Heidegger writes: "In one's concern with what one has taken hold of, whether with, for, or against, the others, there is constant care as to the way one differs from them, whether that difference is merely one that is to be evened out, whether one's own Dasein has lagged behind the others and wants to catch up in relationship to them, or whether one's Dasein already has some priority over them and sets out to keep them suppressed" (BT, 126). A pervasive feature of our consciousness is our incessant measuring of ourselves against others. We are always in competition with the others, even when we have not consciously differentiated ourselves from them. The others dictate what we think about ourselves. "Peer pressure" is not merely a psychological phenomenon. Insofar as we fail to stand in an authentic comportment to our possibilities, choosing instead to measure up to the standards of others, we do not authentically exist. In everyday being-in-the-world, only the others exist: we *are* only in relation to them. "Dasein, as everyday being-with-one-another, stands in subjection to others. It itself is not; its being has been taken away by the others" (BT, 126).

Being-with has three different modes, three forms of "solicitude" or "concern" *(Fürsorge).* The default mode is "indifference," that is, simply passing others by. In the mode of indifference it is not that the others are not there for me, but rather that their being-there is ignored or neglected. The other two modes are "inauthentic concern" and "authentic concern." Heidegger describes the former as the concern that "leaps in" for the other (BT, 122). It is the desire to disburden others of the angst of existence. We intercede in the lives of others to make things lighter for them, all the while, of course, making things easier for ourselves. Without the existential angst of the other disturbing us, it is much easier to repress our own angst. To "leap in" for another is an inauthentic way of caring for him insofar as it entails coaxing him back from his lonely existential perch. In leaping in we encourage the other to lay down his burdens and return to the undifferentiated mass that is the solace of the they-self. Such inauthentic concern, Heidegger explains, fails to recognize the other's existential project, entails treating him like a thing or a "what."

Notice how unsettlingly familiar "leaping in" is. It is a caricature of the ethic of Christianity: Christ takes our burdens upon himself just as we are invited to take up the burdens of others. Heidegger's language becomes particularly acerbic in his vilification of "leaping in"; he calls it a kind of "domination" (BT, 122). We appear to be helping the other when in fact we are enslaving her by making her dependent on us. There are echoes here of Nietzsche's critique of Jewish-Christian ethics as a "slave" morality for naturally inferior types who resent their superiors.

According to the principle of the primacy of absence over presence, "authentic concern" is a modification of "inauthentic concern." Authentic concern is a "leaping ahead" of the other that frees her to face her being, clearing the way for her to assume the burden of her own existence. True concern does not do the other's job for her; it enables her to do it on her own. When authentic concern "leaps ahead" of the other, it salutes her as another Dasein, a "who" engaged in her own unique existentiell project. There is nothing in Heidegger that is remotely close to Christ's commandment to lay down one's life for the other. The act of personal recognition in Heidegger consists of leaving others alone to shoulder their own burden. This rejection of Christian charity emerges from Heidegger's subordination of personhood to a more "primordial" determination. In Heidegger's view, we are not primarily personal beings. Dasein is primordially scattered in its submersion in the they — a collective in the context of which no one is distinct inasmuch as no one has taken the risk to individuate. Heidegger's Dasein is not originarily a person, a "who"; it achieves individuation only through resolute anticipation.

It is something to discover that we are not isolated individuals creating ourselves from the ground up. Such is the hermeneutic situation: we find ourselves thrown into a tradition in terms of which our very identities come to take shape. Heidegger is saying more than this, however; he is making a more evaluative claim. Informed by Luther's vision of man's fallenness — a notion Heidegger takes up in a nontheological register as the habitual self-abasing mediocrity of the human being — Heidegger joins ranks with a long-standing tradition of philosophical elitists, from Plato to Nietzsche. Heidegger is saying in so many words that ordinary people have little capacity for self-government. It is not a far stretch from this observation to the fascist claim that not everyone is entitled to freedom. Some are born slaves. Those who are unfit to rule deserve to be ruled by others.

Back to *Being and Time.* To give a fuller account of the authentic life, Heidegger needs to momentarily transgress his methodological limits — the ethical-political *époche* — and take a detour through the ontic. There is no analysis of inauthentic everydayness possible without an ontic ideal of Dasein. We need to have some sense of what it means to authentically be oneself if we are to understand everydayness as, for the most part, inauthentic. Dasein passes judgment on itself. The self calls us in our everydayness to that which we are not. It calls us to truth, and at the same time condemns our fallen mode of being as untruth. This is the function of "conscience" in *Being and Time.* It is "an appeal to Dasein," a "call . . . to its ownmost potentiality-for-Being-its-Self," a "summoning it to its ownmost Being-guilty" (BT, 269). The authentic self is not something repressed that suddenly bursts through the floorboards in the call. The authentic self is futural for Heidegger. The call comes as something yet to be. The call does not come from beyond the world. It does not come from God. It comes from the futural identity of the self that death alone can give. To understand the nature of this call, Heidegger must give an account of the being of Dasein in Dasein's wholeness. Heidegger needs to describe the existentiell situation that is entailed by Dasein choosing (against the grain) to be itself.

It seems as though the Dasein analytic has assumed authenticity right from the beginning of chapter 1. Heidegger embraces this kind of hermeneutic circularity: the end implicit in the beginning; the beginning only clear in the end. In division 2 of *Being and Time,* to make explicit the ideal of Dasein that has been guiding the discussion, Heidegger must leave the level of the ontological and make an excursus into the ontic, the sphere of living in which we find religious and ethical possibilities for being-in-the-world enacted.[3] How does Heidegger decide which ontic ideal of life is to guide the ontology? Clearly the grounds of the decision must be phenomenological. Religious faith or arbitrary decision cannot help. Only phenomenological evidence of that which most fully actualizes Dasein can have any bearing (given, of course, that Dasein is never fully actual). The ontology cannot rely upon a certain way of being-in-the-world. This is the mistake made by Christian philosophers, a mistake attacked repeatedly by Heidegger. Christian philosophy presumes that ontology unfolds in a certain way on the basis of a disclosure privileged to faith. Heidegger's phenomenology retains this much of the scientific ideal: it proceeds, at least in principle, without religious and ethical presupposition. Whether phenomenology can pull this off is a good question. It is precisely in the context of Heidegger's excursus into the ontic that the whole effort of *Being and Time* to provide a preethical and apolitical analysis of being-in-world threatens to overturn.[4]

Heidegger describes the ontic ideal of authenticity as "resoluteness," but he does not tell us where in the historical and social spectrum of human culture it can be found. We are left with the task of re-

3. See BT, 310: "Is there not, however, a definite ontical way of taking authentic existence, a factical ideal of Dasein, underlying our ontological Interpretation of Dasein's existence? That is so indeed. But not only is this fact one which must not be denied and which we are forced to grant; it must also be conceived in its positive necessity, in terms of the object which we have taken as the theme of our investigation." Further on we read: "Yet where are we to find out what makes up the 'authentic' existence of Dasein? Unless we have an existentiell understanding, all analysis of existentiality will remain groundless. Is it not the case that underlying our interpretation of the authenticity and totality of Dasein, there is an ontical way of taking existence which may be possible but need not be binding for everyone?" (BT, 312).

4. Jacques Derrida has also identified the ontic excursus as the weak point in *Being and Time*. See his *Aporias: Dying — Awaiting One Another as the "Limits of Truth*," trans. Thomas Dutoit (Stanford, Calif.: Stanford University Press, 1993), 80: "Heidegger's chapter on being-toward-death culminates in a series of questions that threaten to bring down the whole edifice that Heidegger was constructing, by mandating the return of what had been so carefully excluded and thereby confirming that ultimately the distinction between the ontological and the ontic cannot be sustained." Derrida goes on to identify the source of ontic importation operative in *Being and Time* as biblical monotheism: "Neither the language nor the process of this analysis of death is possible without the Christian experience, indeed, the Judaeo-Christian-Islamic experience of death to which the analysis testifies."

constructing it for ourselves. Inauthenticity is characterized by "fallenness" into the crowd: by the tendency to make things easy for itself; by avoidance of the burden of living; by allowing itself to be dominated by the opinions and feelings of others; and by suppression of anxiety about death. Resoluteness is walking one's own path, even when others do not approve of or understand you: shouldering the burden of living; suffering the questionableness of existence; and facing the anxiety revealed in certain moods as one's own rightful task. As Heidegger puts it, "We have defined 'resoluteness' as a projecting of oneself upon one's own Being-guilty — a projecting which is reticent and ready for anxiety. Resoluteness gains its authenticity as anticipatory resoluteness. In this, Dasein understands itself with regard to its potentiality-for-Being, and it does so in such a manner that it will go right under the eyes of Death in order thus to take over in its thrownness that entity which it is itself, and to take it over wholly" (BT, 382). Authentic Dasein does not accept at face value the opinion of others. Rather, it rethinks everything for itself. It does not allow itself to be pushed along by the tastes and feelings of the majority, but remains faithful to its unique experiences. It does not let others carry its burden of existence, nor does it presume to carry the burden of others. Resoluteness rises to the occasion of being thrown toward death, recognizing that to shirk this burden would be to lose what alone individuates it. Authentic Dasein does not fly from its impending death, but holds its death before itself as the point on the horizon that unifies its being. Resolute anticipation of death does not make Dasein morbid. On the contrary, Heidegger tells us: it makes Dasein joyful.

What is this ideal of living in a detached but engaged fashion, alive to the moment but never forgetting death, inwardly suffering the burden of one's individuality without mitigating it through superficial enjoyment, courageously persevering in the face of it all? Is it not the ascetic-mystical ideal that emerges predominantly in Christianity (not without significant contributions from Stoicism, Neoplatonism, as well as analogues in the East)? While comparisons with Zen Buddhism are perhaps unavoidable, the differences between the Buddhist path and Heidegger's phenomenology are profound. Dasein is a being-unto-death: its inevitable termination is essential to its identity as an individual irreducibly distinct from all others. The Buddha does not really die; he finds release from the illusion of separate existence. Resoluteness is appropriating one's being-unto-death. Heideggerian authenticity is enacted by the Christian mystic who lives at home in the world because he or she fully shoulders the burden of being human. We should imagine Saint Paul, Saint Teresa of Ávila, the young Luther, and Kierkegaard's "knight of faith" when we endeavor to give shape to Heidegger's ontic ideal (we know from Heidegger's intellectual biography that he was imagining these historical figures). In his earliest lectures he dips into this literature in search of clues to human ontology.[5] The Christian mystical ideal envisions an intensely realized subjectivity, an abyssal inner life fraught with hidden struggles and gnawing doubts — dramatized as "temptations of the devil" — that somehow has not collapsed upon itself, but rather exteriorizes itself in the form of a highly engaged, effective and sensitive individual who is capable of helping other spiritual seekers. The Christian mystic is not an otherworldly freak — eccentricity and antisocial behavior have been frowned upon since the days of the Desert Fathers. The Rule of Saint Benedict, the manifesto for Western monasticism, was written to correct the unhealthy practices that generate such aberrations. The Christian mystical ideal is intended to ground a life that is both entirely given over to the one thing necessary (being-unto-God/being-unto-death) and yet fully present to the moment, with eyes set on eternity and feet firmly planted on the earth. The Christian mystic is a realist with a sense of humor about her own failings, never flippant about the gravitas of living. Above all, she is one who lives in the truth about herself and others and fears nothing more than her own capacity for self-deception. She negotiates a precarious balance between caring and not caring, transparently grounded as she is in the transience of life. She knows that here she has no lasting home or safety. And yet she takes life with the utmost importance, as though everything depended on how she responds to situations that arise. Some find Heidegger's ideal of authenticity morbid. They believe that living in the shadow of death makes

5. On the Christian mystical sources of the early Heidegger, see my *The Early Heidegger and Medieval Philosophy: Phenomenology for the Godforsaken* (Washington, D.C.: Catholic University of America Press, 2006), chapter 5. See also Theodore Kisiel's *The Genesis of Heidegger's* Being and Time (Berkeley: University of California Press, 1993), 69-116.

one somber and morose. A cursory glance at the mystical literature of Christianity shows that this is not necessarily the case. Saint Paul's will to follow the crucified does not make him aloof or sad; on the contrary, he is passionate and brimming over with zest for life. Saint Francis's identification with the poor was a source of irrepressible joy. Heidegger expresses this paradox beautifully: "Along with the sober anxiety which brings us face to face with our individualized potentiality-for-Being, there goes an unshakeable joy in this possibility" (BT, 310).

The most striking difference between Heidegger's resolute anticipation and Christian mysticism is the absence of love *(agapē)* in Heidegger's model. Love for others, with a preferential option for the weak, fragile, and downtrodden, is expressed so powerfully by Saint Paul, Saint Francis of Assisi, and Saint Teresa of Ávila, and is so central to the teaching of Jesus, that it may be called the foundation of Christian life. The Christian practice of self-sacrificial love is key to the mystical overcoming of the sinful ego. Does Christian charity understood in this radical sense fit into Heidegger's analysis? No. Charity understood as *agapē,* self-forgetful love, has no place in *Being and Time.* Authentic Dasein does not carry the burdens of others. It does not lay down its life for its friends. Something has happened to the Christian mystical ideal in Heidegger's formalization.[6] The result of Heidegger's formalization of Christian mysticism is a construct with no place in the history of religion: an immanent ascetic life that no one practices; a God-less secularized mysticism designed by Heidegger to be an alternative to the best his religious tradition could offer. One begins to sympathize with Husserl; upon finishing *Being and Time,* he could not recognize it as phenomenology.

To grasp the political impact *Being and Time* had on its original readership, we must recall the sociopolitical context in which the book was published. In 1927 Germany's efforts at reestablishing itself as a democracy were foundering. The incapacity of the Weimar Republic to deal with runaway inflation and pandemic unemployment was on everyone's

6. Heidegger's ideal bears a striking resemblance to Nietzsche's Zarathustra — another repetition/disfiguration of Western theological models. In spite of Nietzsche's best intentions to re-Hellenize the West, his Zarathustra does not resemble anything Greek; he has walked out of the Bible, a prophet without a God, a Christian without a Christ.

minds. The Marxists were clamoring for a revolution and threatening to pave Germany over with international communism. Nationalistic Germans feared that the culture of Goethe and Beethoven would be amalgamated with Russia into a single classless society. On the other side of the Atlantic, rapacious capitalism was rising in America, bringing with it crass materialism, bourgeois values, and hedonism. Capitalism offered Germany an economic solution to its political problems, a solution that many Germans feared would just as surely as Marxism sound the death knell for their culture. In *Being and Time* Heidegger spoke directly to what his learned readership most feared. He told them their concern for culture was not unfounded: there was something essentially desperate and self-deceptive about the human being. In a situation in which modernity has divested us of traditional bulwarks against mediocrity, we need to think much more defensively about safeguarding those islands of excellence so painstakingly achieved over the centuries.

Heidegger's move into radical right-wing politics should not have come as a surprise to his more careful readers. If the public sphere is constituted by leveling, resistance to excellence, and the domination of averageness, as Heidegger maintains in *Being and Time*, why not abolish civil society? Stop all the sterile chatter about democratic process and give full power to the one who has the courage to act. Enter the bright new political idea, which was seducing Europe in the early twentieth century: fascism. The fascists vilified the liberal state as a moral and political virus, an ad hoc congregation of free individuals who enter into contractual political relations with one another with no intrinsic unity. The fascist state, by contrast, is a "spiritual" entity rooted in the history and destiny of a people. "Fascism" comes from the Latin *fascio,* which means "to bind." What differentiates members of the fascist state from one another pales in comparison to what binds them together: "blood and soil," as the Nazis put it.

The facts of Heidegger's Nazism are as follows. In 1932 the Nazis assumed power by election in Germany. In January 1933 Hitler was appointed chancellor and used the position to seize dictatorial control of all levels of government — including the schools and universities, which had always been public institutions in Germany. The centers of higher learning could no longer count on remaining apolitical. The knowledge industry needed to be brought into alignment with party politics, and for this, new administrators were required. In April 1933 Heidegger was appointed rector of Freiburg University, chosen in effect to spearhead the politicization of the university. Heidegger joined the Nazi Party a month later and remained a party member until 1945. He delivered his inaugural address, the *Rektoratsrede*, on 27 May, under the title "The Self-Assertion of the German University."[7] The address concluded with three vigorous "Heil Hitler's." Heidegger's critics like to point out that he used his power as rector to enforce Nazi ideology in the university and assisted in the denunciation of racially impure colleagues. In spite of his initial enthusiasm for the movement, Heidegger never won the trust of the party, and many of his ideas met with resistance. He offered his resignation on 23 April 1934.

Heidegger spent the war years as a more or less apolitical professor of philosophy, lecturing on the history of philosophy. After the war he refused to comment on his political past. He broke his silence for an interview with the German magazine *Der Spiegel* in 1966 on the condition that it would be published only posthumously.[8] Despite this drama, the interview revealed nothing new, but merely confirmed how entrenched the older Heidegger had become in his denial of guilt. In the interview Heidegger defended his political involvement on two grounds: first, he argued that there was no alternative if he intended to save the university (and science in general) from the anti-intellectualism of mainstream National Socialism; second, he saw an "awakening" *(Aufbruch)* in the National Socialist movement that he believed might be the solution, not only for Germany but also for the West, a view about which he claims to have had a radical change of heart in 1934 after the violence of "the Night of the Long Knives." When read in conjunction with other remarks by Heidegger and his contemporaries, the interview shows that Heidegger understood his error in 1933 as having misread the political situation and

7. Martin Heidegger, "The Self-Assertion of the German University," in *The Heidegger Controversy: A Critical Reader,* ed. Richard Wolin (Cambridge: MIT Press, 1993), 29-39. See also Martin Heidegger, "The Rectorate 1933/34: Facts and Thoughts," in *Martin Heidegger and National Socialism: Questions and Answers,* ed. Günther Neske and Emil Kettering (New York: Paragon House, 1990).

8. Martin Heidegger, "Only a God Can Save Us," in *The Heidegger Controversy,* 91-116.

attributing a world-historical significance to Nazism, which history proved it did not possess. In other words, Heidegger did not have any serious moral or political objection to National Socialism, or to fascism, totalitarianism, and racism.

A reminiscence written in 1940 by Heidegger's student Karl Löwith confirms this reading. Löwith recalls an exchange with Heidegger in which Heidegger admitted that "National Socialism was in agreement with the essence of his philosophy," and that "his idea of historicity was the foundation for his political involvement."[9] Further confirmation of the degree of Heidegger's Nazi sympathies is revealed in a 1945 letter Heidegger wrote to his son Hermann.

> The rectorate was an attempt to see something in the movement that had come to power, beyond all its failings and crudeness, that was much more far-reaching and that could perhaps one day bring a concentration on the Germans' Western historical essence. It will in no way be denied that at the time I believed in such possibilities and for that reason renounced the actual vocation of thinking in favor of being effective in an official capacity. In no way will what was caused by my own inadequacy in office be played down. But these points of view do not capture what is essential and what moved me to accept the rectorate.[10]

Heidegger wanted to elevate National Socialism from its crude "biologism" to something more "spiritual." In 1933 he believed along with many other Germans that in the wake of the collapse of the Imperial powers in the First World War, America and Russia would divide the world between them. Both of these nations were driven by explicitly ma-

---

9. See Karl Löwith, "Mein Leben in Deutschland vor und nach 1933: ein Bericht" (Stuttgart: Metzler, 1986), 57: "[I] told him [Heidegger] that I did not agree either with the way in which Karl Barth was attacking him or in the way [Emil] Staiger was defending him, because my opinion was that his taking the side of National Socialism was in agreement with the essence of his philosophy. Heidegger told me unreservedly that I was right and developed his idea by saying that his idea of historicity was the foundation for his political involvement."

10. Heidegger, "The Rectorate 1933/34," 29.

terialistic visions of humanity. In Heidegger's view, Germany had a unique vocation to preserve and advance civilization through this dangerous moment. The hour had come for Germany to act on behalf of Europe to preserve the spiritual vocation of the West. This would require a political awakening of the people and a mobilization of all levels of German society. Unemployment would be overcome through an act of collective will. The rootlessness of modern life would be countered through enforced common work. The sciences needed to lend their effort by recovering their lost principle of unity and putting a united scientific community at the service of the state. In the 1935 lecture course "Introduction to Metaphysics," Heidegger speaks of the crisis facing Germany as "the darkening of the world." He describes the political situation in vivid terms: "This Europe, in its unholy blindness always on the point of cutting its own throat, lies today in the great pincers between Russia on the one side and America on the other. Russia and America, seen metaphysically, are both the same: the same hopeless frenzy of unchained technology and of the rootless organization of the average man" (IM, 40). The lectures that make up this course were delivered at the University of Freiburg to a roomful of young men, many of whom would be involved in the Nazi war to conquer Europe four years later. At one point in the course Heidegger speaks of "the inner truth and greatness of National Socialism," which he distinguishes from popular Nazism. In the 1953 publication of the lectures, Heidegger added in parentheses after this notorious phrase (without alerting his readers of the interpolation), "namely, the confrontation of planetary technology and modern humanity."[11] The interpolation shows the older Heidegger qualifying his enthusiasm for National Socialism by relating it to his later concern with the question of technology. It is not likely that this is what he meant by the "inner truth" of Nazism in 1935.

The fate of civilization was hanging on Germany's readiness to act. In the dark night of the West, when Germany could no longer count on the old theologies and metaphysics to support it, radical action needed

11. Rainer Marten, letter to Jürgen Habermas, 28 January 1988, cited by Jürgen Habermas, "Work and Weltanschauung: The Heidegger Controversy from a German Perspective," *Critical Inquiry* 15, no. 2 (Winter 1989): 452-54.

to be taken, the justification for which could consist only in "the reso-luteness" with which it was executed. The German nation was called to authentic political action, which means, in the absence of stable identi-ties, "objective truths" or "eternal values" — even at the expense of hu-man rights or the sovereignty of other nations — to decide for itself to be itself. It was not controversial to believe that in 1933 a decision had to be made concerning the future of Germany. What is unique about Heidegger's view of the matter is his conviction that (1) the decision had world-historical consequences; and (2) the German people could no lon-ger rely on any of their traditions for guidance in making it. The decision would have to be a Nietzschean act of creating values in an abyss, surren-dering to absolute leadership of the great ones among us or "choosing a hero," as Heidegger puts it in *Being and Time* (BT, 385).

Whatever Heidegger's reasons for resigning the rectorate, it is cer-tainly true that his enthusiasm for National Socialism waned after 1934. By 1942 he began to see National Socialism as a further sign that the darkening of the world had taken hold of Germany. In his later lectures he voiced some objections to National Socialism — usually cryptically or at least indirectly (Heidegger was never one to agitate his employers). National Socialism, he realized, was not a solution to the crisis of moder-nity but part and parcel of global technology. The führer was no more than a functionary in a technologically driven war machine. Heidegger's work in the late 1930s and 1940s became more and more concerned with the problem of technology and the eclipse of thinking by calculation. This interior defection from National Socialism did nothing to placate the de-Nazification committee in 1945, which wasted no time in revoking Heidegger's license to teach.

Much is made of Heidegger's refusal to recant his radical politics or apologize for his actions and words in the 1930s. While I believe that this "sin of omission," not his actions as rector, is the more serious offense, I cannot help but see the issue from Heidegger's point of view. To recant or apologize would have been to concede that the liberals were right all along and, because his politics was rooted in his ontology, reverse the di-rection of his thinking. Heidegger's refusal to recant is proof that his po-litical actions had an essential relationship to his philosophy. He did not go lightly or unreflectively into political life. While he recognized later that he had made a mistake and backed the wrong horse, the convictions that led him into National Socialism remained largely unchanged after the war.[12]

Heidegger claimed he was never anti-Semitic. He pointed out that during his time as rector, he helped certain Jewish colleagues and students emigrate, for example, his assistant Werner Brock, who found a position in England with Heidegger's intervention.[13] Historians have corrected Heidegger's one-sided account, digging up the unpleasant facts concerning other Jewish colleagues whom Heidegger did not help, some of whom he actively persecuted.[14] Nonetheless, Heidegger's criteria in these matters had little do with race, which he always maintained was a crude category both for politics and for philosophy. The Nazi effort to reduce everything to biology, he believed, was symptomatic of the forgetfulness of being. Like the emphasis on material in Marxism, or capital in capitalism, the Nazi preoccupation with racial resources was another sign of the reign of calculation. For the cultural and intellectual heritage of Judaism, however, Heidegger had little tolerance. As early as 1921 Heidegger was exploring the possibility of removing the Hebraic root from the Western intellectual tradition.[15] Later this would become an obsession: to return to the horizon that opened up with the Greeks and was eclipsed by Judaism, Christianity, and the fusion of Greek and Jewish horizons in the Middle Ages. In the Nazi talk of Aryan supremacy, Heidegger thought the moment had come to rebuild the West from the ground up, a West purified of stultifying Hebraic morality and religion.

Heidegger's political position in 1933 is not accidental to his philosophy but, as he himself suggested to Löwith, is rooted in the ontology of *Being and Time*. The task for the seeker of truth according to *Being and*

---

12. The best commentators on Heidegger recognize the political slant of his philosophy, without using this as an excuse to dismiss the significance of his contribution. See, for example, Otto Pöggeler, "Heidegger's Political Self-Understanding," in *The Heidegger Controversy*, 198-244, at 198: "Was it not through a definite orientation of his thought that Heidegger fell — and not merely accidentally — into the proximity of National Socialism, without ever truly emerging from this proximity?"

13. Hugo Ott's *Heidegger: A Political Life*, trans. Allan Blunden (London: Harper-Collins, 1993), 187.

14. Ott, *A Political Life*, 210-23.

15. See PIA, 123-26; GA63, 17-24; IM, 7-8.

Time is to authentically choose existence, and in a heroic act of self-retrieval and self-consolidation, lift his Dasein above "average" and "fallen" modes of being-in-the-world. Analogously the task for the authentic political community is to choose its existence and raise itself above the self-oblivious everydayness of modern political life. How is Heidegger's politics grounded in his concept of historicity, as he told Löwith in 1936? Dasein's authenticity is bound up with the historical community into which it is thrown, those with whom its destiny is entwined. It must both appropriate the traditions it has been given and strive to authenticate those traditions. In 1933 Heidegger believed that Germany needed to reach toward authentic political leadership in the form of a hero-leader, a führer, who alone could unite the people and overcome Dasein's tendency to shirk its destiny. In an address to the students regarding the 1933 plebiscite to decide if Germany would follow Hitler's lead and withdraw from the League of Nations, Heidegger declared: "The German people has been summoned by the *Führer* to vote; the *Führer*, however, is asking nothing from the people. Rather, he is giving the people the possibility of making, directly, the highest free decision of all: whether it — the entire people — wants its own existence or whether it does not want it."[16]

Fascism offered Heidegger the ideal of a community that is more than a collective of discrete subjectivities, a whole galvanized by a common ethnic origin and political destiny. The fascist hope was to overcome the atomism of civil society. According to the fascist critique of liberalism, the liberal state is at best an institutional check on the freedom of its citizens, a way of keeping them from killing each other. The fascist state, on the other hand, has a positive meaning. The state actualizes the spirit of a people. It fulfills the deepest aspirations of its members and brings into being the essence of the citizen. Fascism ennobles the state with the dignity of subjectivity, the singularity and historical depth of personality, precisely by denying subjectivity of its members. The political unit is not the individual but the state; individuals are depoliticized by means of the subjectification of the state. The individual acts through the state because the political essence of the individual *is* the state.

---

16. Martin Heidegger, "German Men and Women!" in *The Heidegger Controversy*, 47.

Hence the individual apart from the state — either the one who defects from it or the one who never belonged — has no dignity or rights. As Heidegger put it in 1933, "The Führer alone *is* the present and future German reality and its law."[17]

The ontological foundation of Heidegger's politics is found in section 74 of *Being and Time*, "The Basic Constitution of Historicity." The section concerns the facticity of Dasein considered as thrownness into a cultural and ethnic heritage. Facticity is not only being in a world of things and being-with others in a general and undetermined sense; it is above all belonging to a race, a people, a *Volk* with a unique heritage and history. Among its ownmost possibilities, Dasein finds itself fated to belong to a particular, historically individuated people. Cultural-ethnic identity cannot be annulled. If authenticity means to will what you have been destined to be, it entails an appropriation of cultural and racial heritage.[18] A community is united by ethnicity and thrown toward a single fate Heidegger calls a *Volk*, "a people." The self that Dasein needs to will into being is not the isolated, atomic individual of modernity. It belongs to a people.[19] Authenticity is self-emancipation from the they, but it is

17. Martin Heidegger, "German Students," in *The Heidegger Controversy*, 47. Cf. Benito Mussolini, "The Doctrine of Fascism" (1932), in *Communism, Fascism, and Democracy: The Theoretical Foundations*, ed. Carl Cohen (New York: Random House, 1962), 350: "Against individualism, the Fascist conception is for the State; and it is for the individual in so far as he coincides with the State, which is the conscience and universal will of man in his historical existence. It is opposed to classical Liberalism, which arose from the necessity of reacting against absolutism, and which brought its historical purpose to an end when the State was transformed into the conscience and will of the people. Liberalism denied the State in the interests of the particular individual; Fascism reaffirms the State as the true reality of the individual."

18. See BT, 383: "The resoluteness in which Dasein comes back to itself, discloses current factical possibilities of authentic existing, and discloses them in terms of the heritage which that resoluteness, as thrown, takes over." See also BT, 384: "Dasein's primordial historizing . . . lies in authentic resoluteness . . . in which Dasein hands itself down to itself, free for death, in a possibility which it has inherited and yet has chosen."

19. See BT, 384-85: "But if fateful Dasein, as Being-in-the-world, exists essentially in Being-with Others, its historizing is a co-historizing and is determinative for it as destiny. This is how we designate the historizing of the community, of a people. Destiny is not something that puts itself together out of individual fates, any more than Being-with-one-another can be conceived as the occurring together of several Subjects. Our fates have already been guided in advance, in our Being with one another in the same world

not emancipation from all community. A communal belonging together of commonly fated Daseins, authentic concern for the people who share with you the situation into which you are thrown, remains imperative for the authentic life. Since the authenticity of the individual is not independent from the authenticity of the people to whom he or she belongs, it is incumbent upon the individual to work toward the authenticity of that collective. Authenticity can apply to a community only insofar as the community is more than a collective of discrete individuals who have at best ad hoc contractual relations with one another. Inasmuch as Dasein is singularized by its solitary death, a people is singularized by its unique fate. If authenticity is to be predicated of a people, a demos, a *Volk*, it will have to have as the subject of its predication an essentially unified community, a cohesive whole greater than the sum of its parts and singularized by a common destiny, as each Dasein is singularized by death.[20] Dasein cannot pull itself out of this relationship. Heidegger is not speaking merely about the empirical fact of having a certain racial or genetic structure. To be German does not consist in having certain biological features; that is the point on which Heidegger thought the Nazis were mistaken. Germanness, for Heidegger, is not reducible to race even if it is rooted in "blood and soil."

An outline of a politics begins to emerge from *Being and Time,* the politics of a people whose connection is more than a free association, a people who have the capacity, however repressed, to act as a people. Liberal democracy will always be a compromise with the inauthenticity that forecloses this moment of political individuation in the interest of political liberties. The ontological analysis of the being of a *Volk* becomes an ontic program for political action in the 1933 Rectoral Address. The

––––––––––––––

and in our resoluteness for definite possibilities. Only in communicating and in struggling does the power of destiny become free. Dasein's fateful destiny in and with its 'generation' goes to make up the full authentic historizing of Dasein."

20. Cf. Mussolini, "The Doctrine of Fascism," 51: "[Those] who rightly constitute a nation by reason of nature, history, or race ... have set out upon the same life of development and spiritual formation as one conscience and one sole will. Not a race, nor a geographically determined region, but as a single community historically perpetuating itself, a multitude unified by a single idea, which is the will to existence and to power: consciousness of itself, personality."

antidemocratic tone of Heidegger's speech, so shocking on first read, was not particularly scandalous in 1933. Many young German intellectuals were fed up with the weakness and inefficiency of democracy during the Weimar years. Councillor efforts, committee work, and representational government had proven sterile to deal with the social and political chaos of post-Versailles Germany. The moment of crisis required daring leadership. Courageous individuals needed to rise up out of the detritus of German culture, acknowledge that there was no longer anything to be expected from liberal democracy, and risk exposing the nation to an uncertain future. Heidegger envisioned his own ascendancy to the position of rector in this heroic light. Invoking the *Führerprinzip,* Heidegger claims an all-embracing authority over every dimension of university life, which is his by virtue of his courage to claim it.

It is worth noting that the Nazis in the audience did not like the Rectoral Address. Heidegger seemed to be advocating a private National Socialism, without reference to race and the need to politicize the sciences.[21] In fact, Heidegger's politics has striking affinities to Benito Mussolini's style of "spiritual" fascism. For both Mussolini and Heidegger the state is a moral entity, animated by the spiritual destiny of the people, which individuates itself in the form of a single leader, the führer, the corporate man whose mind and heart is identical to the mind and heart of the *Volk.* A movement of such primordial power could not but wreak havoc on preexisting political structures; much would have to be destroyed before anything new could develop. Individuals would need to display great virtue if they wished to contribute to the historical moment. Accordingly, Heidegger calls the university community to self-denial, courage, fortitude, and perseverance. The new era would be born in agony. Manly action and heroic self-sacrifice were needed; the sybaritic middle-class isolationism of liberalism must be eradicated. The university could no longer afford political ambivalence: it is not a passive observer of the moment, but in its vocation as guardian of culture and science, at the very center of the political world. Heidegger calls for faculty and students to make the fate of the nation their own: "The teachers and students who constitute the rector's following will awaken and gain

21. Pöggeler, "Heidegger's Political Self-Understanding," 215.

strength only through being truly and collectively rooted in the essence of the German university. This essence will attain clarity, rank, and power, however, only when the leaders are, first and foremost and at all times, themselves led by the inexorability of that spiritual mission which impresses onto the fate of the German *Volk* the stamp of their history."[22] Mussolini's fascism endorses a similar "spiritual" view of a people, where spirit is not understood in any otherworldly sense, but as the moral character of a people galvanized through historical struggle.[23]

Rector Heidegger is not utopian, but prides himself on his realism. There is no guarantee of peace and prosperity for Germany. All that the Germans could hope for is authentic political life, a genuine corporate personality born of suffering and struggle. "This will to essence will create for our *Volk* a world of the innermost and most extreme danger, i.e., a truly spiritual world." The academic as the epitome of flabby noncommittal intellectual life must now give birth to his better, the worker in the field of knowledge. "The teachers of the university must really advance to the outermost positions where they will be exposed to the danger of the world's constant uncertainty."[24] Bourgeois nineteenth-century society, constituted by the Enlightenment fiction of the solidarity of humankind — which Heidegger calls "a moribund pseudocivilization"[25] — has collapsed upon itself and given way to something immeasurably more concrete: the identity of a people united by heritage and history. Heidegger's

22. Heidegger, "The Self-Assertion," 29.

23. Mussolini, "The Doctrine of Fascism," 52: "The man of Fascism is an individual who is nation and fatherland, which is a moral law, binding together individuals and the generations into a tradition and a mission . . . a life in which the individual, through the denial of himself, through the sacrifice of his own private interests, through death itself, realizes that completely spiritual existence in which his value as a man lies. Therefore it is a spiritualized conception, itself the result of the general reaction of modern times against the flabby materialistic positivism of the nineteenth century."

24. Heidegger, "The Self-Assertion," 34. Cf. Mussolini, "The Doctrine of Fascism," 52: "Fascism desires an active man, one engaged in activity with all his energies: it desires a man virilely conscious of the difficulties that exist in action and ready to face them. It conceives of life as a struggle, considering that it behooves man to conquer for himself that life truly worthy of him. . . . Life, therefore, as conceived by the Fascist, is serious, austere, religious: the whole of it is poised in a world supported by the moral and responsible forces of the spirit. The Fascist disdains the 'comfortable' life."

25. Heidegger, "The Self-Assertion," 38.

language at this point becomes mystical: "The spiritual world of a *Volk* is not its cultural superstructure, just as little as it is its arsenal of useful knowledge and values; rather, it is the power that comes from preserving at the most profound level the forces that are rooted in the soil and blood of a *Volk,* the power to arouse most inwardly and to shake most extensively the *Volk's* existence."[26] The Rectoral Address is a call to a total reorganization of the university, the abolition of academic independence, and the mobilization of the faculty and staff of all departments toward a single political vision. The three "bonds" outlined in the Rectoral Address, "to the national community" *(Volksgemeinschaft),* "to the honor and the destiny of the nation in the midst of all the other peoples," and "to the spiritual mission of the German people," promise to deliver students from the false ideal of freedom, the inheritance of the Enlightenment, and bring them into their true liberty as workers in the field of knowledge. "The much-lauded 'academic freedom' will be expelled from the German university; for this freedom was not genuine because it was only negative. It primarily meant lack of concern, arbitrariness of intentions and inclinations, lack of restraint in what was done and left undone. The concept of the freedom of the German student is now brought back to its truth. In future, the bond and service of German students will unfold from this truth."[27]

In this chapter I have tried to strike a difficult balance between, on the one hand, labeling Heidegger's philosophy as fascistic and, on the other, exonerating Heidegger as having simply made an error in judgment in 1933. I do not deny that Heidegger's thinking is from its root antidemocratic and elitist. Even his style of philosophy, which renounces logical demonstration and traditional argumentation in favor of increasingly oracular pronouncements and makes no effort at reaching scientific consensus, betrays his authoritarian proclivities. Nonetheless, *Being and Time* is not Nazi ideology. On the other hand, Heidegger's fascism is not unrelated to his ontology. Heidegger's politics is the result of a deliberate move from the ontological to the ontic and an application of the Dasein analytic to Germany's political situation. It is not the only politi-

26. Heidegger, "The Self-Assertion," 33-34.
27. Heidegger, "The Self-Assertion," 34-35.

cal application of *Being and Time* possible. And yet the transposition is not arbitrary. In fascist style Heidegger's political speeches assume that the state has its own Dasein, which he elevates above the Dasein of the individual. Everything that is said of the ontic ideal of Dasein can then be directly applied to the state. The product of this troubling transposition is a consistent antidemocratic and antiliberal political platform, which betrays the ethical-political slant of *Being and Time*. Of course, the fit of the Dasein analytic with certain political systems and not others, like its related fit with a certain kind of theology, throws Heidegger's ontological/ontic distinction into question.

CHAPTER 5

Theology

The critique referred to in the title of this book is now gaining momentum and arriving at the place of Heidegger's greatest weakness: his troubled, seemingly intractable, lifelong relationship with Jewish and Christian theology. Heidegger's ontology can be presented with at least a surface neutrality. His ethics and politics, however infamous, are also transparent enough to admit of impartial treatment. Heidegger's relationship to theology, on the other hand, is so convoluted, so shot through with dissimulation and hidden polemic, that it cannot be presented, at least by this author, without a great deal of critical overlay. Contrary to appearances, theology is not a tangential area for Heidegger. Although always behind the scenes, rarely even earning a footnote, theology permeates both the ontology and the axiology of the early and later Heidegger.[1] In two key places Heidegger refers to the dignity of theology (BT, 10; IM, 8). We know from his biography that he knew something about the subject matter. The way Heidegger philosophizes, however, shows a different attitude. In his early work he never misses an

---

1. Karl Löwith saw Heidegger as primarily a religious thinker, offering a post-Christian alternative to theism: "The basis that serves as the background for everything said by Heidegger, and permits many to take notice and listen attentively, is something unsaid: the religious motive, which has surely detached itself from Christian faith, but which precisely on account of its dogmatically unattached indeterminacy appeals all the more to those who are no longer faithful Christians but who nonetheless would like to be religious." Karl Löwith, *Martin Heidegger and European Nihilism,* ed. Richard Wolin, trans. Gary Steiner (New York: Columbia University Press, 1995), 133.

opportunity to polemicize institutional Christianity and its attendant theologies. In the later work he proclaims the advent of a new divinity discontinuous with the history of Western theology, a posttheistic, postcreationist God who heralds the next age of thinking. This apparently neo-pagan inspiration stands in tension with other passages in the later Heidegger in which he is more reticent to speak of the religious. In the technological age, he tells us, no decision can be made either positively or negatively on the question of God: we are so far fallen into the oblivion of being that we can no longer ask about God. We must disclose being by restoring language to its original power before we can presume to speak of God.

Some interpret this impulse in Heidegger's work as a return to negative theology: by saying what God is not, Heidegger clears away the idols that obstruct our experience of true divinity. Without denying that Heidegger's thinking is a kind of hyperbolic *via negativa,* one must make careful distinctions here. To align Heidegger with other negative theologians such as Pseudo-Dionysus, Moses Maimonides, Thomas Aquinas, or John of the Cross is to underplay Heidegger's polemic with the theology of creation; it does not do justice to either Heidegger or negative theology. The architects of the *via negativa* never deny that God is Creator; they deny, rather, any presumption on the part of philosophy or theology to understand the being of the Creator. The distinction between created and uncreated being gives negation a theological imperative; to remove this distinction in an act of maximal negation is to lose the creative tension that animates the *via negativa.* In this chapter I distinguish the early Heidegger's approach to theology from the later Heidegger's approach to the question of god(s). I believe, however, that the continuities between the two periods are as vital as are the differences. Read alongside one another, the early and later Heidegger share an antagonistic relation to Jewish and Christian theology.[2] The early Heidegger's Luther-inspired

2. It should be pointed out that although this position is not without its supporters, it is not the received opinion. The trend is to read Heidegger — especially the later work — as a mystic whose prophetic utterances are, if not Christian, fully compatible with authentic Christianity. Pious Heideggerianism is as old as the writings of Bernard Welte in the 1950s, and as recent as Laurence P. Hemming's widely read *Heidegger's Atheism: The Refusal of a Theological Voice* (Notre Dame, Ind.: University of Notre Dame Press, 2002). My

polemic with Catholicism and scholasticism advocates philosophy's factical Godforsakenness. The post-Christian theology of Heidegger's later work revolves around the notion of a "saving power" concealed in the moment of crisis in the West, and closely related to this, Heidegger's appropriation of Hölderlin's mythology of "the flight of the gods." In both periods an ontology of creation is ruled out.

"Theology we honor by remaining silent about it," Heidegger declares — a dubious honor, to be sure.[3] What Heidegger does not say here (but has elsewhere, in unequivocal terms) is that theology is no longer allowed to speak in the register of ontology. From *Being and Time* we must conclude that Dasein has no experience of God, not even as a direction of desire. Any religious thinker who holds, with Aquinas, a belief in a natural desire of the creature for its Creator *(desiderium naturale)*, which in the human being issues into a rational intimation of the divine, must be corrected by phenomenology. The early Heidegger's hermeneutics of facticity is deliberately "Godforsaken," that is, so lost to the divine that it no longer entertains even a concept of God. It is constructed as a secular complement to Luther's theology of the cross *(theologia crucis)*. According to Luther, reason is so fallen that it no longer has any natural access to the divine. Theology is possible only through a divine revelation that does violence to our fallen mode of understanding. Factical Godlessness, theologically interpreted, is Godforsakenness: the one who lives without God is, from a theological perspective, Godforsaken. In tandem with Luther's assumption of total corruption, the early Heidegger intensifies the Godforsakenness of human existence. The attempt to answer the question of the meaning of being with reference to the Creator is for Heidegger a systematic flight from finitude. Heidegger makes a virtue of the theological poverty of philosophy: bereft of a natural consciousness of God, philosophy is in a privileged position to let the factic speak on its own terms, leav-

---

difficulty with this school of interpretation is that it does violence to Christianity and to Heidegger to make the two fit together. If the later work is read in conjunction with the early writings on theology, as I am attempting here, Heidegger's ambition to go beyond Judaism and Christianity, including its mysticism, is unmistakable.

3. Martin Heidegger, quoted in Ebehard Jüngel, "Gottentsprechendes Schweigen? Theologie in der Nachbarschaft von Martin Heidegger," in *Heidegger. Fragen an sein Werk. Ein Symposium* (Stuttgart: Philipp Reclam, 1977), 42.

ing theology to its proper work of interpreting what it believes to be a divine revelation.

In *The Early Heidegger and Medieval Philosophy* I endeavor to show how Heidegger's enthusiasm for Luther's theology of the cross obfuscates his phenomenology. I trace Heidegger's theological statements back to a surgical act performed in his earliest lecture courses, a delicate removal of the notion of infinite being *(ens infinitum)* from ontology that is so subtly executed that Heidegger's first Christian readers scarcely noticed it. Under Luther's tutelage the young Heidegger came to believe that *ens infinitum* has always led metaphysics into a dead end, from its first suggestions in Plato's notion of the Good beyond being (not quite a Creator, but the source of all intelligibility), to Aristotle's unmoved mover (perhaps not infinite, but certainly eternal), to the medieval metaphysics of the *actus purus,* the Creator who acts not only as the final cause of being but also as its efficient cause, not only the good but also the *ens infinitum.* Heidegger assumes that facticity has never before been properly thematized insofar as ontology has been distracted by the thought of *ens infinitum.*[4] Blinded by a theological idol, philosophy has overlooked the central phenomenon of factical life: temporality. The "horizon for any understanding whatsoever of being" is "time" (BT, 1), or in other words, "being itself is essentially finite" (WM, 108). Human being is therefore not being-toward-the-good, or in the medieval version, a *desiderium naturale* for the *visio beatifica,* but a "being-held-out-into the nothing" (WM, 91). Only on this assumption, Heidegger argues, is it possible to see the being of everydayness in its true colors. On the alternative assumption that being is eternal and infinite — the identity of essence and existence — the being of everydayness is denigrated to a realm of half-real shadows, participatory being that depends upon the infinite in order to be.

In Luther's theology of the cross, nothing short of an irruption of the truth of God into the human world of lies — an event that reconfigures perverse human understanding by gifting it with faith — can redeem us from our corrupt state. God must appear in a form that repulses under-

---

4. See GA61, 108: "With this infinity, life blinds itself, annuls itself. Incarcerating itself, life lets itself go. It falls short. Factical life lets itself go precisely by expressly and positively fending off itself."

standing and forces faith beyond reason into a higher standpoint: the perspective of the crucified. According to such a theology, a philosophy that claims to be purely philosophical, that is, philosophizing as though God had never revealed himself, will be caught in a fallen perspective. Heidegger's view dovetails nicely with Luther's theological skepticism. Philosophy without revelation — if it is genuine and true to its method — is a blasphemy and a theological outrage; it must be resolutely closed to the transcendent, intent upon thematizing the meaning of being human without reference to God. From theology's perspective — Luther's theology — such a philosophy will be both false and true: false in that humanity does not make any sense without God, but true in that an analysis that suspends the revelation cannot but generate such theological senselessness. Heidegger redesigns philosophy in Luther's perspective. Assumptions are made without possible justification, for the means of such justification have been taken away. An analogy for this convoluted hermeneutic structure can be found in pop culture: the half-naked women on the cover of *Cosmo* are not intended for male consumption, but for women. And yet the feminine ideal depicted here — the seductress, eternally young, dying to please the man, yet strangely empowered by this submission — is defined by the male gaze. For such a dissimulation to work, the man's ideal must become the woman's ideal, and the woman's gaze must be abolished. Just as the *Cosmo* view is a woman's image of herself reconfigured according to male desire, so is philosophy's conception of itself colonized by radical Protestantism in Heidegger. Far from being free of theology, Heidegger's early philosophy is always consulting theology, anxiously structuring itself in such a way as to support a certain version of theology while implicitly foreclosing others.[5] And yet it is expressly not intended for theologians, but for philosophers who apparently have freed themselves from theology. Philosophy must be "in principle atheistic," Heidegger says in 1922 (PIA, 121; cf. GA61, 197). Philosophy is "a raising one's hands against God" (PIA, 121 n. 9). "The philosopher does not believe," he writes in 1924 (CT, 1).

5. Notice, for example, the plethora of theological sources cited in the notes to *Being and Time*. For example, introduction, chapter 1, notes ii, iv, vii; division 1, chapter 1, notes i, vii, viii, ix; division 1, chapter 5, note v; etc.

Curiously, the earliest Heidegger (1919-23) admits that philosophy is not a neutral and rational inspection of reality, but a narrative that emerges out of theologically determined situations. "Real philosophy of religion arises not from preconceived concepts of philosophy and religion. Rather, the possibility of its philosophical understanding arises out of a certain religiosity — for us, the Christian religiosity" (GA60, 89). Heidegger explains this puzzling passage in an early letter to Karl Löwith, where he claims that his philosophical work emerges out of his own facticity. To his situation belongs "the fact" that he is "a Christian theologian."[6] Heidegger's sense of factically belonging to the Christian world was short-lived: little trace of it is to be found in *Being and Time.* The sense of belonging to the Christian tradition, even as an atheistic phenomenologist, is nevertheless the motivation behind Heidegger's lectures on religion: the 1920/21 "Introduction to the Phenomenology of Religion" and the 1921 "Augustine and Neo-Platonism" (GA60). The first of these lectures includes breakthrough readings of the phenomenological significance of apocalyptic consciousness in the letters of Saint Paul. The parousia, the second coming of Christ, becomes for Heidegger an index of a formal ontological structure. Heidegger regards New Testament eschatology as the pristine moment in the history of the West when a consciousness of authentic temporality breaks through our otherwise Greek cosmology.[7] Heidegger focuses on Saint Paul's outline of how Christians should live in the interim between the resurrection and the parousia. Paul told the Thessalonians who wondered about the date and time of the parousia that they were asking the wrong questions. The point of living in anticipation of the Christ is not to prepare for a certain moment in the future when Christ will come again. Rather, the Christian should live as though Christ could come at any moment, "like a thief in the night" (1 Thess. 5). Eschatological thinking does not calculate the time between now and the end moment in the future, but rather lives toward the fu-

---

6. Cited in Theodore Kisiel's *The Genesis of Heidegger's* Being and Time (Berkeley: University of California Press, 1993), 78.

7. That I appear to talk here exclusively of "Christian eschatology" is due to the textual restrictions Heidegger places on the subject. It is, of course, the case that the apocalyptic consciousness, which is here identified with early Christian thinking, originates in Hebraic messianism.

ture. Pauline eschatology is the proximate source of the distinction drawn in *Being and Time* between "expecting" and "anticipating" death (BT, 262-63). What we are moving toward in the eschatological paradigm — death, the end of the world, or the second coming — is a return that does not restore the past but repeats the origin in a different way. Eschatology thus breaks with both circular time and linear time. It is a time of unrepeatable moments, but also a time that folds back on itself and recapitulates its beginning: Christ is already and yet he is not yet. The early Christians awaited the recapitulation of the event (the crucifixion and resurrection) that had made them Christians and that would return to them with a new apocalyptic finality in the eschaton, the irreversible end point of history.

Division 2 of *Being and Time* retrieves this paradoxical Jewish-Christian notion of time as being toward the beginning. Heidegger appropriates the "already/not yet" structure of early Christian eschatology under the rubric of "ecstatic horizonal temporality."[8] Dasein does not stand to its future as to a blank space of possibility into which it is pushed from behind by its past. Rather, the future comes toward Dasein as the recovery and confirmation of its past. Anticipating its death, Dasein looks toward the moment when it will fully be, a moment that will never in fact come insofar as Dasein's "self-actualization" is also its impossibilization. In living resolutely toward its future, Dasein comes authentically for the first time into its present. Hence for Heidegger, the ecstatic nature of Dasein (being outside itself, always ahead of itself) indicates the inseparability of the past, present, and future. The self is not a ready-made thing that needs to be uncovered, but a future that is ever coming to be, a call to live in a certain way. The individual cannot know

8. Löwith argues that Heidegger's notion of temporality is based primarily on a "religious . . . and eschatological consciousness." Löwith, *Martin Heidegger*, 38-39. While endeavoring to emancipate itself from Jewish-Christian theology, Heidegger's philosophy remains entangled in Jewish-Christian cosmology. Löwith notes the difference between Heidegger's notion of temporality and Greek cosmology: "How distant is this eschatological-historical thinking, for which everything counts merely as seed-sowing and preparation for an arriving future, from the originary wisdom of the Greeks, for whom the history of time was philosophically insignificant because they directed their view toward eternal beings and beings-which-are-thus-and-not-different rather than toward what is in each case accidental, which could also be otherwise" (39).

who she is until she acquires sufficient experience in life — a past — that can return to her an identity to be affirmed. Life teaches her to recognize which of her past experiences contain the significant "seeds" of her future; the lesson is learned inasmuch as she gives herself over to living through their significance. The past is not available until it comes back as future. She moves toward that which has already been.

It is clear from unpublished notes and numerous references in other early lectures that the proximate inspiration for the young Heidegger's turn to early Christianity is the work of Wilhelm Dilthey. In his *Introduction to the Human Sciences,* which Heidegger studied carefully, Dilthey reveals the roots of "historical consciousness" in early Christian and Reformation theology.[9] According to Dilthey, the religious experience of the early Christian community precipitated a turn away from Greek metaphysics toward spontaneous expressions of the historical self. As the young Heidegger put it, "Christian religiosity lives temporality as such" (GA60, 80). The Christian inversion of the traditional relationship of the human and the divine ("God becomes man") introduces a new understanding of history into the Western tradition. No longer a shadow realm, understood only in reference to eternal ideas, history is reconceived as the real world, the arena of redemption. At the same time subjectivity is given an ontological weight it lacks in Greek metaphysics. The inner life of the early Christians opens up a new order of being, what Dilthey calls "the personal certitude of inner experience of will and heart as well as the content of these experiences."[10] The new attitude to subjectivity distinguishes Augustine's *Confessions* from ancient autobiographies. Socrates' sense of introspection, to "know thyself" as the Oracle at Delphi had commanded, is not historically oriented or factically centered. Socrates is interested only in the timeless essence of the soul, the intellect, *nous,* that which lifts us above the particularities of individual existence to something more ideal, certain, and lasting. In early Christianity the self to be known is not changeless and universal, but singular, concrete, and historical. In Dilthey's view, Augustine's *Confessions* lays

9. Wilhelm Dilthey, *Introduction to the Human Sciences,* trans. Ramon J. Betanzos (Detroit: Wayne State University Press, 1988), 228-39.

10. Dilthey, *Introduction,* 229.

the groundwork for the Western conception of subjectivity as historically situated and temporally enacted.

On the basis of his reading of Dilthey, the young Heidegger con-
cludes that Christian interior experience is not merely a validation of
history but an intensification of it.[11] In the 1921 Augustine course,
Heidegger draws on book 10 of Augustine's *Confessions* to examine the
tension between Augustine's breakthrough to factical life in his notion of
care *(cura)* and his simultaneous covering over of facticity with Neoplatonic metaphysics. Augustine's commitment to Greek metaphysics
makes it impossible for him to resolve the tension between what he is experiencing in himself and what he is reading in Plotinus and Proclus.
Care points to temporality; Neoplatonism points away from the temporal toward the eternal. Augustine comes to know himself only through
the narrative recounting of his own history. His self exists for itself only
in the temporalizing act of giving itself a history. At the very moment of
the breakthrough to historicity, however, Augustine smothers the historical self with Neoplatonic theology: being in its primary sense is the being of the worldless, eternal, uncaused cause, the *summum bonum,* or
highest good. The temporal attributes of human being disengaged in Augustine's *Confessions* are denigrated to shadows of eternity, become not
positive phenomena, but privations of the fullness of being that God
alone enjoys. Augustine resolves the restlessness of human existence
into the *tranquillitas* of the *visio beatifica,* and transfers truth to a realm
beyond history. The early Christian sense of anxious expectation is replaced by Neoplatonic aesthetic possession, and the historicity of the
self, so vividly enacted in the *Confessions,* is buried (see GA60, 118).

Heidegger was also won over by Dilthey's caricature of the scholastic

11. The following statement from a 1919 lecture of Heidegger's could have been written by Dilthey: "The most profound historical paradigm for the noteworthy process of
shifting the center of gravity of factic life and the life-world into the self-world and the
world of inward experience is given for us in the emergence of Christianity. The self-world
as such enters into life and becomes lived as such. What lies forth in the life of the primal
Christian communities signifies a radical reversal of the directional tendency of life. It is
usually thought of as a denial of the world and asceticism. Here lie the motives for the development of completely new contents of expression which life fashions — even up to that
which we today call history" (GA58, 61-62).

age as a time of systematic forgetfulness of history. It is in this context that we should understand Heidegger's letter to Krebs breaking with "the system of Catholicism" on the grounds of insights into "history."[12] The scholastics did not build on the Augustine who had plumbed the depths of the historical self, but on the metaphysician who had fused Christianity and Neoplatonism into a system. Historicity disappears from the tradition for a thousand years until Luther destroys scholasticism. In Luther the repressed self-world of primal Christianity rises up in rebellion to tear down the constructs of metaphysics overlaying it and retrieve historically saturated Christian subjectivity. Against the Hellenistic scholastic "theology of glory," which presumes to know God in the contemplation of nature, Luther declares that "The condition of this life is not that of having God but of seeking God."[13] Heidegger will spend the next decade undoing the medieval forgetting of history by restoring the human being to its temporal horizon. Key to this work is the deletion of God from ontology. In the 1923 lecture "Ontology: The Hermeneutics of Facticity," Heidegger traces the modern notion of subjectivity back to the biblical notion of man as an image of God (*imago Dei,* Gen. 1:26). In Heidegger's view, *imago Dei* is not a phenomenological notion, but at best a revelation and at worst a dogmatic assertion. "Human being was, in a manner cut to the measure of faith, defined in advance as being-created in the image of God" (GA63, 23). Heidegger's intention is to abolish the concept on the grounds that it offers no phenomenological foothold, having emerged as a "closed context of experience" (GA63, 23).

When *Being and Time* was finally published (after several draft versions), the destruction of Christianity and biblical anthropology had lost its urgency for Heidegger. At least in his own approach to ontology, Heidegger believed the work was done: nothing was left of the Creator or the being created in his image in *Being and Time.* The "world," the web of meaningful relations that makes possible culture, science, and language, is horizoned by nothingness. Dasein has no access to anything beyond time, no metaphysical knowledge of the divine, no natural religiousness

12. See p. 10 above.

13. Martin Luther, *Luther's Works,* vol. 25, *Lectures on Romans,* trans. Walter G. Tillmanns and Jacob A. O. Preus (St. Louis: Concordia, 1972), 225.

111

or consciousness of God. The terms of this position change somewhat after *Being and Time,* but the nontheistic orientation remains the same. In this reconfiguration of Western ontology the question of God, and the related question of the ultimate good, can no longer be asked.

Commentators have noticed, however, that Christian theology continues to determine key sections of *Being and Time,* albeit in a concealed manner. Heidegger draws on biblical texts and Christian mysticism for the sake of understanding being-in-the-world, and yet insists that Dasein's *existentialia* have no religious lineage. Theological texts that appear to corroborate existential structures, such as "fallenness," "being-unto-death," "conscience," and "being guilty," are dismissed for their lack of primordiality.[14] Contrary to appearance, Heidegger says, these structures originate in purely philosophical experience.[15] What are we to make of this? Here I will offer only a few observations.[16] First, Heidegger's work attests to the power of religious experience, particularly Jewish and Christian religious experience, to disclose basic features of being-in-the-world; assuming that there is more than crypto-theology going on in *Being and Time,* this means that there is either something basically religious about human life or something penetratingly phenomenological about certain religious authors — or perhaps both. Second, Heidegger's "methodological atheism," if intended as an effort to think

14. See, for example, BT, 190 n. iv; 235 n. vi; 306 n. ii; 338 n. iii.

15. "Heideggerian thought was not simply a constant attempt to separate itself from Christianity.... The same Heideggerian thinking often consists, notably in *Sein und Zeit,* in repeating on an ontological level Christian themes and texts that have been 'de-Christianized.' Such themes and texts are then presented as ontic, anthropological, or contrived attempts that come to a sudden halt on the way to an ontological recovery of their own originary possibility." Jacques Derrida, *The Gift of Death,* trans. David Wills (Chicago and London: University of Chicago Press, 1995), 22-23. Cf. Fergus Kerr, *Immortal Longings: Versions of Transcending Humanity* (Notre Dame, Ind.: University of Notre Dame Press, 1997), 47: "Heidegger's attitude to Christian theology, hostile at one level, overtly and explicitly so, attributing the monstrous invention of the transcendental subject to Christian theology, is also proprietorial, indeed exploitative of and even parasitical upon Christian theology.... It may be said, without much exaggeration, that almost every philosophical innovation in *Sein und Zeit* may easily be traced to a theological source."

16. For a more developed critique, see S. J. McGrath, *The Early Heidegger and Medieval Philosophy: Phenomenology for the Godforsaken* (Washington, D.C.: Catholic University of America Press, 2006), 1-24, 203-7.

being free of religious assumption, fails from the beginning; far from thinking independently of his religious context, Heidegger works with ideas that, according to his own early study of Christianity, depend upon their original religious context. It is no wonder that Heidegger's phenomenology has proven to be such a powerful inspiration to twentieth-century theology: the theologians were having their own material given back to them translated into phenomenological terms.

The final act in the drama of the early Heidegger's entanglement with theology (although not his final word on the question of God) is the 1927 essay "Phenomenology and Theology." The text originates in a lecture Heidegger delivered to the Marburg Faculty of Theology. After several years of close collaboration with the biblical theologian Rudolf Bultmann, Heidegger felt a need to bid farewell to academic theology. In "Phenomenology and Theology" he offers definitions of ontology and theology intended to show the proper working relationship between the two "sciences." The tension between Heidegger's sympathy for authentic theology and his simultaneous commitment to philosophical unbelief tears the text apart. Heidegger is trying to maintain incompatible positions. On the one side he argues, in the medieval spirit that regards philosophy as "a handmaid" to theology, for a theologically independent ontology providing philosophical foundations for theology. Philosophy, then, is relinquished from theological influence while theology is given to enjoy a more limited freedom so long as it sticks to its proper terrain: divine revelation. The relationship is not between equals: theology is answerable to philosophy on certain questions, but philosophy, provided it ventures no theological claims, is in no way answerable to theology. While few theologians are likely to accept these terms, the position is at least coherent. Heidegger then confuses matters by arguing that philosophy and faith cannot avoid conflicting with one another and therefore must face each other as mortal enemies.[17] Considered in this light, it seems to Heidegger that philosophy is not entirely neutral on the ques-

---

17. See GA9, 53: "This peculiar relationship does not exclude but rather includes the fact that faith, as a specific possibility of existence, is in its innermost core the mortal enemy of the form of existence that is an essential part of philosophy and that is factically ever-changing. Faith is so absolutely the mortal enemy that philosophy does not even begin to want in any way to do battle with it."

tion of faith, but rather actively opposes it: philosophy lives out of an existential unbelief. This second claim is much closer to the view of radical Protestant theologians such as Karl Barth, who reject any theological deferral to philosophy and insist that theology cannot surrender the ground of its thinking; it must make ontological claims. The criterion for testing the truth of ontology must be internal to theology; it cannot be imported from unbelief. Heidegger does not appear to recognize any incompatibility between these two models of the relationship.

Like other positive sciences, the basic concepts of theology arise on the ground of an unclarified preontological understanding of being. The subject of theology is the mode of being-in-the-world determined by faith, which Heidegger, drawing on the nineteenth-century theologian Franz Overbeck, calls "Christianness" *(Christlichkeit)*. Theology is the conceptual interpretation of Christian existence. Presumably this definition is advanced to avoid any possible overlap with ontology. Faith is the only way to access the "revelation of revelation." Theology is thus the ontic science of faith. By "faith" Heidegger does not mean either propositional belief or vague religious hope but "the believing-understanding mode of existing in the history revealed, i.e., occurring, with the Crucified" (GA9, 45).

Without taking theological issue with this conception of theology, one can still ask on what grounds Heidegger privileges it in his phenomenology. What gives phenomenology the right to dictate what is and what is not authentic in theology, especially since, by Heidegger's own admission, it has no understanding of theology's subject matter? The answer is found in Heidegger's finitization of being. Since being no longer has anything to do with the divine, theology can have nothing to say on questions of ontology. Theology cannot even qualify the concept of being it uses in theological discussion in the light of revelation (as Augustine and all who followed him in the Middle Ages did). Theology must presume being, just as all the positive sciences do. Because being is the theme of another science, the positive sciences must accept ontology on authority. If philosophy declares that being is finite and has no analogical likeness to the divine, then theology cannot dispute it. In a reversal of the medieval understanding of the relationship of theology to philosophy, theology works within the boundaries established for it by philosophy.

Despite Heidegger's intention to restore theology to its true dignity, he portrays it in terms that neither Luther nor Aquinas would accept. For Luther, theology has the power to negate everything philosophy says, including its ontological claims. For Aquinas, theology listens to philosophy on matters of ontology, but retains a power of veto, for the revelation gives it a divine measure that exceeds anything found in philosophy. Prescinding for a moment from the Lutheran rhetoric of "Phenomenology and Theology," we see that what is going on in this essay is theologically intolerable: unbelief setting the agenda for theology. Under the guise of an effort to understand the dignity of theology, Heidegger is declaring war on it, making it in effect impossible. If philosophy and theology are indeed mortal enemies, then the position for which Heidegger advocates is theology's enemy dictating the terms of theology's surrender.[18]

Although his polemic against the notion of divine creation goes back to the early Freiburg lectures, Heidegger only fully defines the problem as "onto-theology" much later. At the same time, he begins to soften on questions of religion. The later Heidegger lifts the moratorium on religious talk and aims his critical remarks at "the God of metaphysics," the *causa sui,* who is posited as a foundation of being. Onto-theology, the causal genealogy of beings back to a first cause, is the central plot of

18. Heidegger makes his growing hostility to theology plain in the 1930s. See IM, 6: "Anyone for whom the Bible is divine revelation and truth has the answer to the question 'Why is there anything rather than nothing?' even before it is asked: everything that is, except God himself, has been created by Him. God himself, the uncreated Creator, 'is.' One who holds to such faith can in a way participate in the asking of our question, but he cannot really question without ceasing to be a believer and taking all the consequences of such a step. He will only be able to act 'as if.' . . . On the other hand a faith that does not perpetually expose itself to the possibility of unbelief is not faith but mere convenience: the believer simply makes up his mind to adhere to the traditional doctrine. This is neither faith nor questioning, but the indifference of those who can busy themselves with everything, sometimes even displaying a keen interest in faith as well as questioning. What we have said about security in faith as one position in regard to the truth does not imply that the statement 'In the beginning God created heaven and earth' is an answer to our question. Quite aside from whether these words from the Bible are true or false for faith, they can supply no answer to our question because they are in no way related to it. Indeed, they cannot even be brought into relation with our question. From the standpoint of faith our question is 'foolishness.' Philosophy is this very foolishness. A 'Christian philosophy' is a round square and a misunderstanding."

Western metaphysics, which for Heidegger consolidates technological thinking. The God of this story is not the true divinity but merely a principle necessary to the structure. "This is the Cause as *causa sui,* and this is the just and proper name for God in philosophy. Man may neither pray to this God, nor may he sacrifice to him. Confronted by *causa sui* man may neither sink onto his knees nor could he sing and dance" (ID, 65).

The critique of onto-theology comes to the fore in the posthumously published 1936 manuscript *Contributions to Philosophy* (GA65), the 1946 "Letter on Humanism," and the 1957 lecture "The Onto-Theo-Logical Constitution of Metaphysics" (ID, 33-67). In these texts Heidegger breaks his earlier theological silence and speaks of how the divine might enter into philosophy without philosophy falling into onto-theology.[19] Only by overcoming calculation through the destruction of onto-theology can we hope to create the conditions for the "nearing" of the holy. Objective presence, enshrined as ontological criterion through its apotheosis in God, the most present and objective of all objects, must be displaced so that the spontaneity of *physis* is permitted to show itself. No longer needing a Creator to ground beings, which emerge from the nothing "without a why," Heidegger turns to the divine to understand it on its own terms. In a chapter of *Contributions* entitled "The Last God," Heidegger appropriates Hölderlin's thesis of "the flight of the Gods." For Hölderlin, the last god of the old world was Christ; after his departure, we await a new god whose identity is obscure. The religiosity of modernity is marked by a romantic longing for the departed divinity, a feeling of having lost that which is most precious. Heidegger transposes Hölderlin's romantic theology into a post-Christian context. When we find ourselves homeless in the world technology has made for us, and the earth is no longer a site for the in-breaking of the Holy, when the gods have departed, we await the advent of "the last god."

19. For example, in *Contributions* he writes: "Considered according to metaphysics, god must be represented as the most-being, as the first ground and cause of beings, as the un-conditioned, in-finite, absolute. None of these determinations arises from the divine-character of god but rather, from what is ownmost to a being as such, insofar as this is thought as what is constantly present, as what is objective and simply in itself and is this, in representing, explaining, attributed as what is most clear to god as ob-ject" (GA65, 308).

The last god has its most unique uniqueness and stands outside those calculating determinations meant by titles such as "mono-theism," "pan-theism," and "a-theism." "Monotheism" and all types of "theism" exist only since Judaeo-Christian "apologetics," which has metaphysics as its intellectual presupposition. With the death of this god, all theisms collapse. The multitude of gods cannot be quantified but rather is subjected to the inner richness of the grounds and abgrounds in the site for the moment of the shining and sheltering-concealing of the hint of the last god. The last god is not the end but the other beginning of immeasurable possibilities for our history. For its sake history up to now should not terminate but rather must be brought to its end. We must bring about the transfiguration of its essential and basic positions in crossing and in preparedness. Preparation for the appearing of the last god is the utmost venture of the truth of being, by virtue of which alone man succeeds in restoring beings. (GA65, 289)

Metaphysics/technology/onto-theology are coming to an end. The darkening of the world that heralds this end is also the stillness that precedes the dawning of the new epoch. The last god's arrival heralds the beginning of a postmetaphysical age of thinking. Why is he last? The last god is the unexpected messiah who comes at the end of a series of here unnamed divinities, the gods who have overseen the rise and fall of the West. The new sending of being that he initiates will free us from calculation and send us into a fresh experience of truth. Philosophy's task is to prepare for this unconcealment. In the 1946 "Letter on Humanism," Heidegger speaks in a similar vein of ontology humbly clearing a space for revelation despite being unable to presume the name of the divine. Being, which both summons us and depends upon us, is not God. But without a true notion of being, the question of God cannot even be asked. Ontology must resist deciding for or against God. It can no more be atheistic than it can be theistic. It must acknowledge "the boundaries that have been set for thinking" (LH, 254).[20] Insofar as it truthfully articu-

---

20. See also LH, 252-53: "With the existential determination of the essence of man, therefore, nothing is decided about the 'existence of God' or his 'non-being' no more than

lates the human situation, ontology clears away obstructions to the experience of divinity, even if that divinity is still to be unconcealed.

The removal of the notion of creation from ontology is the centerpiece of this preparatory work, a posttheistic thinking that leads neither to teleology nor to absurdity. Teleology is the study of being that recognizes within an entity an end that defines it, the essence of a thing, what it is good for, that for the sake of which all its attributes exist. The teleological view is the horizon for the language of divine creation: God is the one that gives every essence its telos. He has designed creatures so that they do certain things, they actualize certain potencies; when you have genuinely named what they do, you have articulated the idea in God's mind that precedes the being of the thing. According to Heidegger, this view has dominated our philosophical and scientific thinking since Plato. Heidegger also avoids the fall into absurdity, which is a reverse teleology. In Sartre and Camus, things have no essence, no sense; without God, being is nauseatingly absurd. This reaction against teleological thinking is negative creationism; it concedes to theism that meaning depends on a Creator who puts a telos into things. The later Heidegger's notion of *physis* as that which spontaneously emerges into presence breaks both with the theistic idea of nature as an effect of God's creative act and with the atheistic notion of nature as a meaningless clot of matter in motion. Heidegger wishes to restore something of the wonder, which is older than teleology and absurdity, *that* things exist.

Where Heidegger once proclaimed the necessary atheism of philos-

---

about the possibility or impossibility of gods. Thus it is not only rash but also an error in procedure to maintain that the interpretation of the essence of man from the relation of his essence to the truth of being is atheism. And what is more, this arbitrary classification betrays a lack of careful reading. No one bothers to notice that in my essay 'On the Essence of Ground' the following appears: 'Through the ontological interpretation of Dasein as being-in-the-world no decision, whether positive or negative, is made concerning a possible being towards God. It is, however, the case that through an illumination of transcendence we first achieve an adequate concept of Dasein, with respect to which it can now be asked how the relationship of Dasein to God is ontologically ordered.' If we think about this remark too quickly, as is usually the case, we will declare that such a philosophy does not decide either for or against the existence of God. It remains stalled in indifference. Thus it is ultimately concerned with the religious question. Such indifferentism ultimately falls prey to nihilism."

ophy and refused to discuss the religious, in 1946 he lambastes modern indifference to the sacred:

> Only from the truth of Being can the essence of the holy be thought. Only from the light of the essence of divinity can it be thought or said what the word "God" is to signify. Or should we not first be able to hear and understand all these words carefully if we are to be permitted as men, that is, as ek-sistent creatures, to experience a relation of God to man? How can man at the present stage of world history ask when he has above all neglected to think into the dimension in which alone that question can be asked? But this is the dimension of the holy, which indeed remains closed as a dimension if the open region of being is not cleared and in its clearing is near man. Perhaps what is distinctive about this world-epoch consists in the closure of dimension of the hale [*des Heilen*]. Perhaps that is the sole malignancy [*Unheil*]. (LH, 253-54)

The last sentence is a play on the German verb "to heal," *heilen* (related to the English "hale" and "hearty"), and its etymological relation to the German word for "the holy," *das Heilige. Das Unheil* means "calamity" or "doom." The calamity and sickness of the age is its loss of a sense for the holy. To heal *(heilen)* the age means to draw near to the holy once again. We should read these passages from the "Letter on Humanism" alongside the last paragraphs of "The Question concerning Technology," where Heidegger speaks of a "saving power" lying in potency at the heart of technology. Heidegger's talk of a "saving power" at the center of the danger (QT, 340) thwarts any tendency to misinterpret his critique of technology as a renunciation of modern science and technology; retreating to some premodern style of living is not a solution. Somehow, we need to find the potency for health that is hidden in Western dis-ease. That which is sickening us must be transformed in its essence so that it becomes a source of health. Like grace in Christian theology, the saving power is "unexacted," unconditioned by any human act, incalculable; it comes to us wholly from without.

The later Heidegger's mystical style hearkens back to his earliest research on medieval mysticism, especially his fascination with the German medieval theologian Meister Eckhart. In some of his earliest notes Heidegger remarks that mystical union in Eckhart is accomplished through "letting be," or *Gelassenheit*.[21] For Eckhart, *Gelassenheit* means letting go of self-will and letting God irrupt from within.[22] We do not have to clear a space for God to enter the soul; God is already within us. We have only to let go of a false notion of ourselves, the belief that the self is the master of itself and its world. *Gelassenheit* means that the mystical union is not something we do, but something we let be done. Heidegger's preoccupation with Eckhart's notion of *Gelassenheit* returns in the 1949 *Memorial Address* (GA16). He distinguishes calculation from "meditative thinking," which waits for beings to show themselves, and contemplates "the meaning which reigns in everything that is." Thinking waits patiently, like the farmer, "for the seed to come up and ripen." It is relaxed and open and lets beings show themselves as they are. As the breakthrough to the God within is achieved in Eckhart by not-doing, so the breakthrough to being in Heidegger is a letting go of the grasping and control of calculation. It is in this context of endeavoring to cultivate *Gelassenheit* that we should interpret Heidegger's oft-quoted remarks from the 1966 *Der Spiegel* interview: "Only a god can save us."[23]

In the 1951 essay "Building Dwelling Thinking" Heidegger advances his most positive claims regarding the divine, introducing a posttheistic icon of the whole: "the fourfold." The whole is a unity of two sets of opposites: "earth" and "sky," "mortals" and "gods." The earth is the dark, self-withholding ground of being; the sky is the illumination of being, a place of light and space. Mortals are beings-unto-death; the gods, the deathless ones, are "the beckoning messengers of the godhead" (BDT, 351). Mortals have a unique destiny to shepherd the fourfold. When we emerge from our technological bind and become free from calculation, we will reawaken our calling as Dasein to be the cleared site for the

21. See the 1917 note at GA60, 309.

22. Eckhart writes: "Where the creature ends, there God begins to be. Now God desires nothing more of you than that you go out of yourself according to your creaturely mode of being and let God be God in you." *Meister Eckhart: A Modern Translation*, trans. Raymond B. Blakney (New York: Harper and Row, 1941), 127.

23. *The Heidegger Controversy: A Critical Reader*, ed. Richard Wolin (Cambridge: MIT Press, 1993), 91-116, at 107.

emergence of beings into presence and, therefore, the ones uniquely in the position to safeguard the essences of things. This is what it means to "dwell." We let beings be what they are by renouncing calculation and practicing *Gelassenheit.* As things show themselves in their coinherence in the whole, the whole itself becomes unconcealed and "the gods" draw near once again.

Hans-Georg Gadamer points out that Heidegger's principal preoccupation throughout his long career was the question of the divine.[24] Heidegger's personal, professional, and philosophical difficulties with the Catholicism of his upbringing shaped and directed his efforts to find a new language to speak of God. His later posttheism is closely related to his early objections to philosophical theology. Indeed, it is with respect to theology that the unity of the early and late Heidegger is most striking. The early work is primarily destructive: removing the Western idols that make it impossible to experience or think the truly "divine God." "The gods" who constitute one side of the divine quaternity ("the fourfold") cannot be taken literally; Heidegger is not naively neo-pagan. Nonetheless, Heidegger's doctrine of the gods is of questionable value to anyone genuinely concerned with the future of Western religion. By rejecting the Hebraic and Latin roots of the West, Heidegger has jettisoned the living sources of our civilization. He retreats to a beginning that never happened — "the Greeks" before they were Greek — and constructs a "primordial" origin of the West after the pattern of his own prejudices.

24. Hans-Georg Gadamer, "Being Spirit God," in Hans-Georg Gadamer, *Heidegger's Ways,* trans. John W. Stanley (Albany: State University of New York Press, 1994), 183: "[W]hat that might mean, to speak of God — this was the question that motivated him [Heidegger] and pointed out his way of thinking."

Why I Am Not a Heideggerian

Heidegger has single-handedly resurrected the study of ontology in the twentieth century; for this reason alone he deserves the place he has earned in the Western canon. Heidegger's undoing of the Cartesian-Kantian critical turn in philosophy — a turn that replaced metaphysics with epistemology and ontology with transcendental psychology — shows that the problems of metaphysics have not been solved. Indeed, by grappling with metaphysics, however inconclusively, philosophy advances deeper into its essence. For Heidegger, philosophy is not a "hard" science on a progressive path to knowledge, leaving in its wake a succession of solved problems. Philosophy is a way of life. The endless circling around unanswered and unanswerable questions constitutes a specifically philosophical mode of existence. When it is faithful to its call, Heidegger tells us, philosophy does something superbly human: it interrogates being, and in that very act proves that the human being transcends being in some inexplicable sense. Heidegger has his doctrines and claims, but his influence is more keenly felt not where he has succeeded in winning disciples, but where he has inspired and agitated others into radical philosophizing. Heidegger did not so much start a school as a style of thinking marked by a refusal to capitulate to received interpretations and a commitment to lay bare the conceptual architecture underlying a given philosophical idea. Thinking against Heidegger has proven a fruitful endeavor. Without their polemics with Heidegger, there would be no Levinas or Derrida.

As frequently as Heidegger is praised in such terms, he is also vilified for his Nazism. In all fairness to a complex man, Heidegger did change his sociopolitical views, however subtly. Heidegger's post-Nazi sociopolitical musings on technology assume an identification with the human community that could have been a significant labor only for someone as ill-disposed to his "fellow man" as Heidegger was. He probably felt that this was apology enough for the errors of judgment he committed in the 1930s. In the later work, Heidegger's rhetoric of destiny (common to every period of his thinking) expands from his narrow focus on Germany to a transnational embrace of "the West," "man," and finally, the ecological community under the metonym "the earth." A few illustrations comparing the early to the later Heidegger on this point should suffice. In *Being and Time,* we read that "authentic care" for others means setting them free to be themselves, letting them carry their own burden instead of dragging them down to some common level. The later Heidegger speaks of "sparing" or letting all *things* be themselves. Setting free, which previously was confined to relationships between human beings, has now expanded to include the nonhuman. In *Being and Time* we read about being-in-the-world as the fundamental existential of Dasein. The later Heidegger speaks of Dasein as "dwelling on the earth," which, whatever else it might mean, cannot be reduced to the human world of tools and projects.

Notwithstanding these significant shifts in emphasis in the later Heidegger, my critique hinges on sociopolitical oversights in Heidegger's work that are structurally repeated in his polemic with Christian theology. The intuitive reader will have concluded that I am some kind of personalist, some kind of humanist, and some kind of Christian. This philosophical/theological orientation preceded my doctoral work on Heidegger; what I discovered in Heidegger only confirmed and allowed me to refine it. By ruthlessly attacking it, Heidegger continually reminds me of what, if anything, I still hold sacred. Christian reactionaries (Catholic and Protestant), antimodernists, conservatives, and fundamentalists have the opposite effect on me: rather than "building up" my faith, they leave me with less than I had before. Heidegger, on the other hand, awakens me to the urgency of an ever-present need to review, reappraise, repeat, or reject my deepest convictions. To what degree am I willing and able to own the philosophical and theological traditions that have governed my education, thinking, and spiritual life since I began to speak? By so violently overthrowing them Heidegger forces me to choose: Will I follow him or some other post-Christian prophet, or will I hold on to something that I deem too precious to surrender, something that perhaps has been misrepresented, and that I am not only willing to own but also ready to defend?

Heidegger's attack on Christianity occurs behind the scenes, shielded from view (and critique) by the screen of the distinction between the ontological and the ontic. "Existentiell" comportments such as authentic Christian faith are not in question, Heidegger says, so long, of course, as they never presume to be ontologically founded. Heidegger's distinction between the ontological and ontic is at best contrived, at worst, a strategy for advancing, without argument, questionable ethical, political, and theological positions. He himself cannot maintain the distinction but transgresses it repeatedly: by interpreting Dasein's average everydayness through the lens of an unnamed but sovereign "ontic ideal"; by privileging a radical Protestantism over his native Catholicism through foreclosing theological options; and finally, and most damagingly, by political ventures, which only proved, in a humiliating way, how far from the purity of a neutral ontological investigation he was. The impossibility of a methodological distinction between an ontological and an ontic investigation does not deny ontological difference. It is, rather, a hermeneutic point. If the way into the ontology is truly through the ontic, then ontology cannot claim title to first philosophy. That is not to say that ethics is first philosophy, or that theology has regained its lost preeminence; it is to say that philosophizing is far too hermeneutically complicated to structure in this way. There can be no firsts here: everything must happen at once because it has always already happened. It is no surprise that the early Heidegger has no resources to resist authoritarian politics; he finds himself endorsing National Socialism in the 1930s as a consequence of his ontic commitments: specifically, having rejected certain pillars of Christian humanism: the sacredness of the common, the dignity of the person, and the human being's openness to God. To conclude, then, a brief word on Heidegger's relation to each of these.

Being and Time is driven by a not-so-subtle denigration of commonness. The rule of the many is the rule of the mediocre; the average man generates nothing exceptional. Heidegger's doctrine of truth, or *aletheia*, subordinates verification and judgment to apprehension, elevating the vision of the single thinker above the consensus of the community. From "the common man," who does not distinguish himself in any way, or "the common space," where "the they" congregate, nothing can be expected except infectious mediocrity. Society, commonness, and the public sphere each "tempt" Dasein into making things easy for itself, mitigating the difficulty and solitude of authenticity, and smothering the call of conscience with noisy chatter. Heidegger seems to be missing something here, something that other writers, for example, G. K. Chesterton or even David Hume, point out with passion and wit: the personal quality of common life. The small talk that facilitates our day-to-day interactions with our neighbors, no matter how trivial and unconscious, is still *personal.* When I ask my next-door neighbor "How are you?" I may not be terribly interested in the answer, but the form of expression is intimate, a salute to his "subjecthood," the hidden world that only he can disclose. The regulars in the local pub are perhaps weak and unexceptional people. But they are fellow human beings, and when I join them for a pint in the late afternoon I express my solidarity with them. I understand something of their small pleasures and their big disappointments. In our ritual celebrations of the tragicomedy of our common humanity, we are neither a faceless mass nor isolated monads: we are a community, and what we share is more significant than what divides us.

According to the medieval tradition, a person is an irreducible center of intellection and volition constituted by relations to other persons. Modernity corrects the medieval tendency to subordinate the personal to the ontological by introducing the unprecedented notion of "subjectivity" into the philosophical lexicon (a move the significance of which Heidegger repeatedly underplays). Hegel tells us how the "I" is only fully herself when she is recognized by another "I."[1] This happens in a dramatic way in the experience of love, but it also happens in quotidian ways, for example, when the girl behind the cash register in the local

---

1. G. W. F. Hegel, *Phenomenology of Spirit,* trans. A. V. Miller (Oxford: Oxford University Press, 1977), par. 178: "Self-consciousness exists in and for itself when, and by the fact that, it so exists for another; that is, it exists only in being acknowledged."

store is recognized by a customer in some small and seemingly negligible gesture as not a machine but a person, with her own hidden inner life that infinitely exceeds the menial role she has been forced to assume as "counter help." The full showing of her personhood is obstructed by the role economics forces upon her; it cannot be directly expressed behind the counter, but neither can it be entirely concealed from other persons.

A provisional, "formally indicative," definition of dignity: dignity is humanity recognizing itself and so raising itself into full dialogical and reciprocal actuality. Dignity comes from the Latin noun *dignatio,* which means graciousness. The verb, *dignor,* means to recognize something as worthwhile. Note that *dignatio* depends on the other; it does not merely subsist in a person like an objective quality, nor does it exist in isolation from others. One does not testify to one's own *dignatio;* rather, *dignatio* is recognized in you in the same act by which it is shown to you. Dignity is ineradicably dialogical; it requires a situation of mutuality. The concept, so overused (a clear example of "idle talk"), has, despite its intrinsic vagueness, taken two millennia to develop. In the Middle Ages *dignus* was the excellence that accrued to an individual by virtue of his or her divinely bestowed office. For Aquinas *dignus* was an attribute of kings and queens.[2] The modern political concept is an expansion to the point of reversal of the medieval notion: dignity in the contemporary sense is an ineradicable and universal phenomenon. The Enlightenment leveled medieval social hierarchies, as the Reformation had leveled ecclesiastical hierarchies a century before. What was thought to be a divinely bestowed privilege became the common possession of all: in the "enlightened" view we are each of us kings and queens.

The Enlightenment did not invent the notion of universal dignity; it secularized a Jewish notion, one that could not fully develop until the

---

2. In the *Summa Theologica,* question 122, article 2, Aquinas asks, "Whether it belongs to observance to pay worship and honor to those who are in positions of dignity?" Aquinas's answer highlights the distance that separates the medieval from the modern: "It belongs to persons in positions of dignity to govern subjects." Dignity, in Aquinas's view, is not something common to all, but rather the privilege of the few. It is a mark of excellence or superiority, peculiar to those whom God has placed above others as natural rulers. Kant's advance in this regard should not be overlooked: it is only with Kant's ethics that the irreducibility of subjectivity becomes foundational for the concept of "humanity."

collapse of the Middle Ages and the Hellenistic hierarchies so central to medieval thinkers. The notion of universal dignity is the secular face of the Jewish doctrine of the *imago Dei*. Man and woman, Genesis tells us, are made in the image of God (Gen 1:27). The notion of *imago Dei* must be understood in relation to Jewish iconoclasm if its full significance is to be understood. The Jews are forbidden from making an image of God in wood or stone. God is wholly transcendent and ineffable: no created being can represent him. And yet the human being, in some unfathomable way, images him. If the person alone among all creation, and by virtue of his or her individuality, images God, how can dignity be denied him?

It is legitimate to ask what exactly images God in the human being. Some traditional answers include "rationality," "freedom of will," or "language." The problems arising from these too-narrow definitions of human dignity (and every definition is too narrow, inevitably excluding someone who must not be excluded) encourage a more indeterminate answer: the most we can say is that at "the core" of the human being resides a mystery that images the divine. Like the tabernacle in the Jewish Bible, the human being is a site for the unveiling of God. We are answerable for guarding and keeping safe this sacred space. Dignity needs two to be manifest; we cannot take dignity from another; we can only, in some way, abolish the manifestation of dignity between us by refusing to recognize it. Dignity is not earned, nor can it be lost. It cannot be reduced to an acquisition or an achievement. It has nothing to do with capacities (here Kant erred). It is not reducible to rationality or the ability to act morally. It cannot even be reduced to the capacity to relate. The severely retarded, who suffer a diminished capacity to relate to others, retain their dignity. If it is not something that they can express through word and action, others must express it for them by treating them with dignity: the community takes up the burden of the incapacitated or disadvantaged; they *dignify* them by expressing their humanity for them. If the community fails to carry them in this way, it degrades itself.

Far from annulling dignity, the violation of the sacred site of the divine image by acts of evil reinscribes its irreducibility. Moral outrage maintains the sacredness of the human; this has been the role of "Holocaust literature" in twentieth-century theory. The Nazis systematically dehumanized their victims; they stripped them, sheared them, starved them, routinely beat them, invented obscene techniques to punish and execute them. What is truly astonishing about the Holocaust is the tremendous trouble and expense the Nazis took to dehumanize the unwanted. They might have won the war if they had seduced the "inferior races" into supporting their effort. On occasion Nazi camp leaders invented miserable jobs without any purpose other than to systematically wear away the inmate's very human tendency to take pride in his labor. Nazism was an effort to prove that dignity is not "inalienable," that it can be taken away, that the inmate could be so brutalized that he loses his humanity. The inmate was to become so obsessed with getting a mouthful of bread and avoiding blows that he was driven to indifference to the suffering of others, or best of all, enlisted in the work of brutalizing his fellow inmates.

Heidegger's antihumanism, which impelled him to reject a priori any notion of human dignity, made him a ready ally for fascism. One thinks of Jacques Maritain's understanding of fascism as a political ideology predicated on the denial of universal dignity.

Fascism has as a metaphysical root an absolute pessimism of a rather volunteeristic and Machiavellian sort. Practically, it denies that man comes from the hands of God and that he retains within him, in spite of everything, the grandeur and dignity of such an origin. This pessimism, which invokes incontestable and empirical truths, turns these truths into lies because it is indifferent to the fact that man comes from God. . . . Not God, but the state will create man. The state, by its constraints, will oblige man to come forth from the nothingness of the anarchy of the passions and lead an upright and even heroic life.[3]

Regarding "being-toward-God": no topic is more susceptible to banalities, none more disfigured by sentimentality and trivial interpretation. Theological silence is not necessarily a bad idea, as Aquinas knew, especially where certain words have become meaningless through overuse: words like "love," "redemption," and "sacrifice." Nevertheless, the silence of the saint before the infinite chasm that separates him from his

3. Jacques Maritain, *Scholasticism and Politics* (London: Geoffrey Bles, 1945), 10.

God is something other than Heidegger's theological moratorium. Whatever God is, the question to which he represents an answer is too axial and fundamental to be ruled out by philosophy. Current trends in French phenomenology show that no amount of Lacanian psychoanalysis, deconstruction, and critical theory can abolish the theological question from philosophy. Wherever philosophy is free to be itself, it asks about God as spontaneously as children pray.

If "the saving power" truly grows at the heart of the danger, if the medicine is in fact a property of the poison, then, according to Heidegger's own thinking, Christian humanism cannot be simply abandoned. Heidegger's effort to think the history of the West without Christianity, the Judaism out of which it developed, or the humanism that grew out of it, weakens his entire project. Ad hoc approximations of Eastern ways of thinking, reconstructed neo-paganism — the proclamation of new gods — cannot be the solution. The eco-technological crisis requires us to rethink who we have become, to look into the history of the West for the sake of opening new ways of being modern while remaining authentically ourselves. What is the West? Is it Greek? Is it Jewish? Is it Christian? Will we access the history of the West by treating its dominant ethical-theological paradigm as something that was added on and can be taken away by great iconoclasts like Nietzsche and Heidegger? Or is it our Christian heritage (the historical fusion of the Hellenistic and the Hebraic) that is precisely our destiny? A thought that eludes Heidegger, however germane it may be to his hermeneutics of facticity, is the ultimate reason why I cannot be a Heideggerian: Christianity is not finished with us.

Index of Names

Aquinas, Thomas, 3, 11, 13, 15, 17, 44, 61, 68, 80, 103, 104, 115, 126, 128
Arendt, Hannah, 5
Aristotle, 1, 4, 5-6, 8, 9, 11, 15, 34-35, 38, 57-58, 59, 62, 63, 65, 70, 73, 76, 105
Augustine, 44, 65, 107, 109-11, 114

Barth, Karl, 22, 91n.9, 114
Braig, Carl, 12n.10, 18
Brentano, Franz, 31, 56
Bultmann, Rudolf, 21, 113

Camus, Albert, 118
Caputo, John, 75, 76n.12
Cassirer, Ernst, 14
Chesterton, G. K., 125

Derrida, Jacques, 85n.4, 112n.15, 122
Descartes, 4, 16, 28, 30, 31, 39, 40, 62, 63, 64, 69
Dilthey, Wilhelm, 109-10

Eckhart, Meister, 54, 120
Erfurt, Thomas, 12n.11, 58

Francis of Assisi, Saint, 88
Freud, Sigmund, 4, 64-65

Gadamer, Hans-Georg, 5-6, 25, 121

Hitler, Adolf, 20, 89, 90, 95
Hölderlin, Friedrich, 24, 74, 75, 104, 116
Hume, David, 3, 125
Husserl, Edmund, 8, 16, 17, 19, 21, 28-33, 35, 40, 54, 56, 58, 64, 69, 77, 79, 80, 88

Jaspers, Karl, 25, 26n.29

Kant, Immanuel, 4, 12, 14, 36, 54, 64, 65, 66n.8, 69, 80, 81, 122, 126n.2, 127
Kierkegaard, Søren, 21, 34, 48-50, 54, 87
Krebs, Engelbert, 10, 12, 13, 111

Lask, Emil, 15n.16
Leibniz, Gottfried, 4
Levinas, Emmanuel, 81, 122
Löwith, Karl, 91, 94, 95, 102n.1, 107, 108n.8
Luther, Martin, 14, 17-18, 21-22, 34, 42, 44, 54, 64, 84, 87, 103-6, 111, 115

Marx, Karl, 4, 89, 94
Marx, Werner, 62
Mussolini, Benito, 96n.17, 97n.20, 98, 99, 99n.23, 99n.24

Nietzsche, Friedrich, 4, 14, 16, 24, 78, 80, 83, 84, 88n.6, 93, 129